J·U·S·T
SAY NO

By Larry Kramer

FICTION

Faggots

PLAYS

Sissies' Scrapbook
The Normal Heart
Just Say No
The Furniture of Home

SCREENPLAYS

Women in Love
The Normal Heart

NONFICTION

Reports from the holocaust:
the making of an AIDS activist

Larry Kramer

J·U·S·T
SAY NO

A Play About

a Farce

ST. MARTIN'S PRESS   NEW YORK

Design by Judith Stagnitto

Library of Congress Cataloging-in-Publication Data

Kramer, Larry.
    Just say no / Larry Kramer.
      p.   cm.
    ISBN 0-312-03371-0
    I. Title.
  PS3561.R252J8   1989
  812'.54—dc20   89-32748

First Edition

10 9 8 7 6 5 4 3 2 1

NOTE TO THE READER

All names, places, characters, and incidents have been imaginatively framed, and any resemblance to actual events, or to persons living or dead, is in the eye of the beholder.

The playwright acknowledges his gratitude, with love, to Morgan Jenness, Rodger McFarlane, and Nick Olcott for their help and encouragement during the writing of *Just Say No*, and to his attorney, Leon Friedman, who showed him how it could all be said.

THE FARCE IN
JUST SAYING NO

You've got to have rocks in your head to write a play.

You must be a masochist to work in the theater and a sadist to succeed on its stages.

And you must be retarded to believe you can support yourself.

These tenets apply to any and all playwrights. But particularly to those who have anything important to say.

Playwrights, of course, are nuts anyway. I think it's ten times harder to write a play that works than a novel, and a hundred times harder to write a play than a screenplay. Screenwriting is craft, not art (and group craft at that), and novelists have all the time and pages in the world through which to leisurely maneuver their investigations.

Playwrights have two or three acts, two and a little more hours, and about a hundred pages, to create an entire world containing a certain kind of truth, to peel away the pain within the pain within the pain and hit the jugular.

What makes a good play? Oh, there are lots of theories. A

strong clothesline that keeps pulling an audience along while it unconsciously asks, and the writer quite consciously answers: "What next?" "Now what?" Tension. What goes on between the lines. The tension in relationships between characters. The tension between characters and events. The tension between the characters and their actions, and the audience. The tension between what the playwright tells you and what s/he doesn't tell you. The tension between what you are told and what you are thinking. The tension between ideas and actuality. The tension between right and wrong.

Conflict. All of drama is fights. Fights between conflicting needs, desires, ideas.

I don't think there's any playwright who sits down and consciously applies all these pretentious formulas I've just listed. Though that's what possibly comes out, we sit down and write because we simply want to say something.

That's much easier to deal with, isn't it? I want to say something. I want to tell you about my mother and father. I want to tell you about my childhood. I want to tell you this story I heard. I want to tell you about this unusual character. I want to tell you the world is awful—or wonderful—or funny—or sad. I want to tell you what I think about something. I want to tell you what it's like to be gay. (Did you want to hear that one?)

And I believe the resolution of all this must be moral. Very unfashionable, morals. Very out of season, morality.

Most of what today's critics acclaim as good plays bores me greatly. These plays are thin, trendy, banal, plain, pointless. They bear little relevance to the life I am living or have lived. I don't respond to the tensions and the conflicts and the "what next"s. I find few characters challenged—at least in the way I understand challenge. I don't leave the theater enlightened. Or angry because I've been forced to confront something I don't want to think about but should. These plays are about people I don't want to know. These characters and the world they inhabit not only bear little relation to my life or my dreams, they don't even arouse my curiosity. And I am a pretty curious guy.

And the writers of these plays rarely present a point of view or a resolution—or a moral—that isn't banal. These plays add nothing important to life and to the world. Why should I waste my time attending them?

Until recently, good plays were also about language. They weren't composed in words of one syllable. Or in dialogue so aching to be street-smart accurate (or Jewish suburban or minority ghetto—though black playwriting of late often has been more interesting than white playwriting) that a heritage that includes Aeschylus, Sophocles, Shakespeare, Shaw, and Williams might never have existed. Once upon a time, heightened language reached for the same stars as big themes and noble conflicts. Until Beckett and Pinter and their bastard offspring came along and diminished what was said. Why do we now settle for so little? Beckett didn't destroy the theater of language; that was done by the critics who so slavered over his work that it became unfashionable to pursue other possibilities. That is, if you wanted a good review and desired to be included in college curricula. Critics like to be trendy, like everyone else. And God knows Americans—and particularly New Yorkers—like to be trendies.

It seems to me that the more a play is *about* something—an opinion, a philosophy, a specific point of view—the more the critic feels bound to attack it. The modern play, to be "artistically correct," must not take sides, ruffle feathers, churn up waters, make you think. It must also not be about "others," because that makes the trendies uncomfortable, unless it is about the poor or downtrodden, which allows trendies to condescend. It definitely must not be critical of the status quo—i.e., the trendies themselves; we are not a nation good at either criticizing or laughing at ourselves. Once upon a time, Gustave Flaubert (with Joyce, the altar trendy critics worship at in the world of Novelty, as they kiss poor Beckett's ass in the world of Play) maintained that a writer must be careful not to intrude too personally into his characters' lives, action, and thoughts. *"Ne pas conclure"* ("Draw no conclusions") was his motto and "You should write more coldly" was his advice. These somehow became the definitions, the highest goals, the boundaries of modern writing. Distance. Objectivity. Observation without authorial intrusion.

Well, if you read Flaubert, you will find that he is just as intrusive and opinionated and selective and manipulative and emotional an author as the many great ones who preceded him. But because critics have said *"Ne pas conclure"* and "You should write more coldly," It Must Be So, and writers have been pulverizing their brains and their talent ever since, as, with determination, they actually extract their juices from their work. Imagine writers trying to make their writing less interesting! But that is exactly what is considered good writing today. The word and deed flattened, lest they be too orotund.

It is no different in the theater. Thirty-five years ago, Walter Kerr wrote a book, *How Not to Write a Play*, which pleaded (obviously to no avail) for a return to heightened and poetic theater—language and ideas and challenge. Shaw, Ibsen, Chekov, Aeschylus, Sophocles, Shakespeare: remember them? They would probably be out of work if writing today. TV and tabloid critics would bemoan "wordiness" and "length" and "author's message" and "too complicated plot" or "lack of action." Meanwhile raving about plays where characters have no opinions, take no sides, give and/or lose nothing of import. Where there is no conflict, only petty obstructions. Where nothing of life and death is at stake. Where there is no *drama*.

Might as well stay home, thee and me. Which most audiences now do. And watch TV.

Theater should astonish, amaze, frighten, shock, purge, touch, and move. (Here I go again.) Make you angry. Make you cry. Make you laugh. Help you learn. Inspire. All of the above. That's what it used to do. That's what it started out to do. Intentionally.

Once upon a time the theater was the home of opinion and anger. (Not only drama, but tragedy, farce, and comedy can be very angry.) It was actually meant—can you believe it?—to rouse the public and create discussion and change the world. Sophocles and Shakespeare and Marlowe and Pirandello and Racine even dared to criticize rulers and kings. Aeschylus actually dared to question the gods. What's the last American play where our "rulers" were taken to task? Or a religion challenged? Congreve and Wycherly and Goldsmith and Sheridan and Marivaux and Wilde dared to satirize the ruling classes. What's the last American play you saw that dared to do that?

American theater reflects an inordinate inability to laugh at ourselves, to criticize any powers-that-be. How exceptionally boring. And polite.

Theater today is polite and boring. Compared with what's available everywhere else—movies, television, fiction, non-fiction, rock videos, magazines, street corners, Central Park, even journalism and daily newspapers—theater is terribly polite and boring. No wonder audiences stay away in droves.

When something comes along that is offensive, and is meant to be offensive—actually aggressively affronting current thinking; actually struggling with determination to crash through a brick wall of apathy or denial or ignorance—today's theater of boring politesse is now so entrenched, and the critics now say "You must write more coldly" so automatically, that what should be the true nature of the playwright's calling is not only overlooked, *it* is found to be offensive. The playwright's true task is now viewed, by critics and their desperate-to-be-led-into-trendiness audiences alike, as a different kind of breech: a breech of taste, of the status quo, of politesse—the very tepid qualities the playwright, if he or she is any good, should be trying to blast off an audience's shoulders like the leaden, scurvy dandruff it is.

The last time the American theater was healthy—through the 1920s and 1930s and 1940s (and don't give me that hoary argument that now there's TV and all sorts of other distractions for our leisure time: people inherently love to go out)—plays were about issues and ideas and interesting people and danger and conflict and *the world* (as against the contemplation of the playwright's navel). These are some of the people who wrote plays then: Lillian Hellman, Robert E. Sherwood, Clifford Odets, Goerge S. Kaufman, Moss Hart, Edna Ferber, Maxwell Anderson, Elmer Rice, Eugene O'Neill, Arthur Miller, Philip Barry, Sidney Howard, Sidney Kingsley, William Saroyan, Paul Osborne, S. N. Behrman, George Abbott, Ben Hecht, Charles MacArthur, the Marx Brothers, John Steinbeck, P. G. Wodehouse, Thornton Wilder. And I'm not even touching the musical, or foreign writers whose work was produced here, such as Sartre, Anouilh, Coward, Maugham, Shaw, Pinero, Priestly, O'Casey.

Sort of makes you realize how stinking the paucity is now, doesn't it?

The opinionated play published herein is *about* something. About something that may murder millions of people, that is murdering tens of thousands of my fellow gay men, and is possibly set to murder me. I was not surprised when a number of New York critics slaughtered me. I'm accustomed to that by now. By now I have learned that I rarely get good reviews, and that critics don't review what Larry Kramer writes or says, they review what Larry Kramer is, which is a homosexual. And they review what they think of homosexuality—they don't like it— or what they think homosexuality should be—they don't like it the way it is—and they aren't very interested in hearing what I, or any other gay writer, has to say about it. When Neil Simon writes an autobiographical play, they don't review his life, or his heterosexuality; they review his play; but that's because critics are heterosexual, too, or maintain they are. So they don't have to confront anything. Or be challenged. Or lead the way. They can just sit back on their politesse.

Wouldn't it be the most boring world if everything and everyone were alike? And if everyone wrote the same play?

The theater now is the most boring place in the world. And everybody *is* writing the same play.

What I was most surprised by in the reviews for *Just Say No* was the amazement a number of critics registered that I really thought plays could change people's minds, *accomplish something*. Help change the world for the better. How dare I have harbored such a thought! And written such a play!

But I do believe this. Oh, I do believe it so.

And so should the critics.

That's what art started out to do. Once upon a time. Back in those once upon a times when criticism, too, was considered an art, and to serve art.

I am certainly not the first nor will I be the last writer to complain bitterly that bad critics destroy creativity and understand little about it. I get angry that reputedly comprehensive heterosexual publications have yet to give me—or most other gay writers—really good reviews. By "good" I mean thoughtful. Considered and considerate of what we are trying to say. We don't mind being criticized; we do mind being blindly attacked by bigots, or relegated to thumbnail assessments in the back pages, or—most likely—totally ignored and unreviewed at all. There are many fine openly gay writers writing about gay subjects now. Our novelists include Andrew Holleran, David Leavitt, Christopher Bram, Paul Monette, Gary Indiana, Rita Mae Brown, Sarah Schulman, Gary Glickman, Edmund White, John Rechy, Dorothy Allison, Brad Gooch, Dennis Cooper, Michael Nava, May Sarton, James Purdy, Gene Horowitz, Krandall Kraus, James McCourt, Armistead Maupin, George Baxt, Allan Garganus, Paul Bowles. Our playwrights writing about gay subjects include Victor Bumbalo, William Hoffman, Terrence McNally, Harvey Fierstein, Doric Wilson, Robert Patrick, Charles Busch, Martin Sherman, Albert Innaurato, Robert Chesley, Joseph Pintauro, Lanford Wilson, Arthur Laurents. How many of them have you read or seen? How many of them have you tried to understand? If you find depiction of gay life, particularly gay sex, foreign, does it ever occur to you that we often find depictions of straight sex and heterosexuality foreign?

It is exceedingly painful to face the fact that, over the years, I know that such treatment has taken its toll on me, and on every other gay writer. (And, for that matter, on every "minority" writer.) And that I would have been a more productive artist if I didn't have to withstand all the diatribes hurled at me because few critics, and the publications they write for, have empathy or interest in homosexuality and what it's like to be gay in this world. It rankles to see all the second-rate straight white males who churn out dreck year after year get all the recognition, the best-seller lists, the Broadway hits, the Tonys and Pulitzers and National Book Awards, the movie sales, when I know I and other gay writers are better writers and thinkers than a lot of them and we are treated so dismissively, if we are noted at all. Such positioning also turns many of us to other endeavors completely, or into bitter men and women, from either fighting a fight that seems never to be over, or—even more debilitating—ceasing the struggle altogether.

Sour grapes, you say? Well, as my best friend fielded my fear that this entire essay might be construed as filled with nothing but: "Those folks tried to kill you, honey; you're due a few sour grapes."

The New Yorker does not consider gay literature a category worthy of discussion. Nor does *Esquire*. Or any of the literary quarterlies—the *Paris Review, Antaeus, Grand Street*, and their like. *The New York Review of Books* does not appear to believe that such a thing as homosexuality even exists. *Vanity Fair*, despite the existence on its staff of many gays, seems to me to be so homophobic as to often come close to actually breaking laws against slander. The same can be said of *The Nation*. *The Village Voice* rarely reviews gay books and plays. *Time* never and *Newsweek* infrequently. And, for publications located outside of New York, gay writing simply does not exist.

The New York Times does occasionally nod our way. But it is a condescending nod: reviewers are rarely equipped for the task. Would you give a book on electrical engineering to a florist to review? Would a feminist manifesto be fairly treated at the hands of a misogynist? The *Times* often appears to go out of its way to locate a reviewer ludicrously removed from a sensitivity toward gay subjects. My recent non-fiction book on AIDS was reviewed by someone completely unfamiliar with this epidemic and its effects on my community. But then I have never had a considered review in *The New York Times*. Yes, I am still sucking on a few sour grapes.

But gay artists try not to. We try to reason with ourselves that it is the creation first and foremost that is most important —not its reception by a world. Perhaps there will be acceptance after death—now much closer for too many of us. Because of a growing network of gay bookstores and an increase in the number of gay community theaters, our work does reach an audience that supports us, financially and emotionally, little by little and more and more. My family may think, from reading and viewing what they read and view, that everything I've written is a flop; but in the gay world I have made a certain higher mark.

But there is no writer who can accept relegation to a ghetto happily. Like any other writer, we want to be universally heard. We want you to try to understand what we are trying to say to you. If we are widely panned and even more widely ignored, how are we to get our message out? We want gay playwrights chronicling our history to reach the acceptance of, say, August Wilson.

Gay writers try hard to avoid the paranoid scenario: the straight world does not want us to get our message out. Stomp us into oblivion and there will be no gay literature to attend to. At its worst, we have come to see this attitude exemplified in our government's inattention to AIDS. Perhaps it will go away, or perhaps they will go away, we now know to be the subtext of what's going on. Harvey Fierstein spends twelve years trying to get *Torch Song Trilogy* produced, before finally putting it on himself. David Leavitt gets clobbered, in *Vanity Fair*, not for what he's written but for what he hasn't written, because the homosexuality he's writing about differs from the homosexuality the critic, James Wolcott, wants to read about. Every second-rate heterosexual playwright and filmmaker gets invited to the Eugene O'Neill Theater Center or Robert Redford's Sundance Institute, but not openly gay ones dealing with openly gay subject matter. Every major New York play agent—fourteen of them—turned down my play about AIDS, *The Normal Heart*.

By the time the AIDS epidemic came along and I knew I had to write about it, I'd learned many of the above lessons. AIDS was not being, and has not been, attended to because it occurs in populations the majority isn't interested in and find expendable. Just as the media had, traditionally, brutally treated gay artists and their work, so had the media shown a remarkable lack of interest in covering this devouring epidemic.

I've come to realize that most critics, reporters, and journalists (there is often very little difference among the three) are, along with what they write, and whom they write it for, painfully conservative in bias. So here comes AIDS—a medical mystery so complicated as to make it very difficult to make comprehensible in sound bites, in short paragraphs, and certainly not without first carrying out a great deal of digging, research, and homework. The press has been very reluctant to do this research and homework. Consequently, most of the many AIDS scandals just aren't written about.

And our ideas of what is truly scandalous unfortunately often involve the heterosexual majority. If some think AIDS was allowed to fester and grow unattended in New York because they believe its Mayor is a closeted homosexual terrified of being revealed as such if he be found too attentive to the demands of the city's gay population, how in the world do you get the straight press to report this suspicion? If some think AIDS was allowed to further fester and grow unattended on a national level because they believe our former President and his First Lady were fearful lest various sexual scandals and proclivities in their own pasts and their own family be revealed, how in the world do you get the straight press to report these suspicions? These are valid suspicions—that sexual hypocrisies have more to do with the conduct of the affairs of state than historians allow. But "straight" leaders "protect" themselves by erecting unwritten codes of decorum—if you will, politesse—that an increasing number of gays do not support. There is no actual law that prohibits naming a public official as homosexual, or that constrains a press from revealing a boisterous heterosexual life—no law, that is, except the unwritten ones: it is considered by heterosexuals as bad taste.

But gay people do not consider it bad taste to be identified as gay. In fact, huge numbers of us consider it exceedingly prideful. And exceedingly, tragically, unhealthy to conceal it. This has become brutally apparent as such hypocrisy allows so many of us to be so casually put to death.

Such, indeed, is the message, the moral, of *Just Say No*.

And such, indeed, is the continuing unwillingness of the heterosexual world to hear a message so unpleasant to them that they will do everything in their power—including their continuing ignoble attempts—at stifling our creative voices in any and every way they can.

In 1973, my first play, *Sissies' Scrapbook*, was produced. In those days, Playwrights Horizons was not so handsomely ensconced in its Forty-second Street home; rather, it shared space with a dance company at the old YWCA on Eighth Avenue and Fifty-third Street, and all its plays were put on in an old gym, with bleachers for seats. The entire budget for the five performances (extended to eight) allowed by Actors Equity (because nobody got paid anything) could not have been more than several hundred dollars. I had a wonderful cast, the audiences were exceptionally responsive, I felt my play was appreciated and my message understood. Critics did not review these "showcase" productions in those days; though I wrote to Clive Barnes, then a *Times* critic, he did not respond or come to see it. When the play closed, there seemed no hope for further productions. Since I then supported myself primarily as a screenwriter, I went back to the movies.

But I was hooked. I kept remembering: I had moved people. I'd made them cry. *Something I had written* had been able to touch the audience. After each performance, I could see them leave the theater crying. Some of them would seek me out, still in tears. I had made people feel what I had felt, for my characters, for their stories, for what had happened to them. Heady stuff. No movie I had ever written had provided me with that experience. (Anyway, movies don't work in the same way. Movie actors don't create their performances from interaction and tension with an audience. That doesn't lessen their effectiveness or usefulness—as entertainment. But it's a hard medium through which to convey *ideas*, and as I have said, I think good plays should contain a large dollop of good ideas. And it's ideas that change the world, not entertainment.)

A year later a producer appeared who offered to produce *Sissies' Scrapbook* commercially Off-Broadway. During two weeks of previews, again people were moved: I saw them crying. Despite a production inferior to the first one, and despite my inability to solve to my satisfaction a structural defect, something was still working. The play was about four men who had been best friends since their days together at Yale. The producer objected to the original title and *Four Friends*, an inadequate substitute, was used. But the play was still about cowardice and the inability of some men to grow up, leave the emotional bondage of male collegiate camaraderie, and assume adult responsibilities. Three of the men were straight and one of them was gay. They all were cripples in one way or another and one of the straight ones did indeed become actually crippled in Act Two.

This was to be my first experience of extending to the straight world—and straight men—messages they did not wish to hear. I received a brutal clobbering from the *Times*. Clive Barnes, who arrived half an hour late, began his review with: "With friends like these you don't need enemies." Despite other and more encouraging reviews, the producer closed the play on opening night. "The *Times* closed it," the producer said to me. "You can't beat the *Times*."

We now come to an unfortunate fact of life with which I've been told even the *Times* itself is uncomfortable—the disproportionate influence of a *Times* review on the run of a play. Although they had also disliked the film of D. H. Lawrence's *Women in Love* which I'd scripted and produced, and they were to be vitriolic toward my novel, *Faggots*, which came out in 1978, a movie and a novel can eventually outrace bad reviews: the former because film companies spend fortunes in advertising to dispel all bad words, and the latter by the very fact that a small volume of printed pages can somehow stay around for a long time and find its own audience. But a play rarely survives a bad *Times* review, particularly without an enterprising and/or rich producer. This kind of producer is now exceptionally rare. And foolish, because by now the public, those trendies, has handed over responsibility to the *Times* for making theatrical judgments for them. A bad review more than not elicits the reaction: thank goodness—another play I don't have to see.

I did not suffer my failure well. I had witnessed the slaughter of my child and it hurt too much. And back in the movie business, I was confronted once again by another painful obstacle: movies are not interested in what I am interested in. Increasingly aware of my gay identity, I wanted to write about that. Film companies are even more homophobic than theater critics. To this day, there has never been a good American film financed by a major studio about homosexuality, despite the fact that every studio has more than its share of gay executives, producers, stars, and writers—even, in some cases, the very studio heads themselves.

When I knew I had to write about AIDS, I found I had no choice but to return to the play form, for several reasons. I knew no film company would finance such a movie. It had taken me three years to write my novel and I was obsessed with the notion that my AIDS message had to get into the world quickly. It also seemed to me that only the play form could provide the sense of *immediacy* I felt essential.

I also thought the play form was the best way to get matters attended to. Ed Koch and Ronald Reagan would have no choice but to pay attention to AIDS after opening night of *The Normal Heart*. Yes, I conceived of the theater as a means of achieving something politically. I was going after Koch, and Reagan, and—courageous me—*The New York Times*. My soap box was planted firmly on the ground of Joe Papp's Public Theater and Joe Papp is as good a producer and attention-getter as there is. And although I might suffer critical clobberings again, I knew Joe guaranteed us an eight-week run.

Why was I going after *The New York Times*? Because, along with Koch and Reagan, they shared an ignoble disdain for AIDS. Their early reporting was rare and grudging. In the first nineteen months of the epidemic, as the number of cases rose from 41 to 958, they allowed only seven articles into its pages, and never on Page One. During the three months of the Tylenol scare, in 1982, the *Times* wrote about it a total of fifty-four times. Four of these articles appeared on the front page. The total number of Tylenol deaths: seven.

I cannot tell you if the *Times* critic Frank Rich liked *The Normal Heart*. I think he was conflicted. On the one hand, my play criticized the hell out of his employer. On the other hand, my play was about dying young men. Even he wasn't that cruel as to totally crucify a play about dying young men. The day after he came to see it, the *Times* called for two tickets for that evening's preview. In those seats sat William Honan, their cultural affairs editor, and a lawyer with a flashlight. Every time the *Times* was mentioned in the play, the flashlight would go on and the lawyer would write down the line. When Rich's review appeared, appended to it was a short announcement from the editors denying the charges I'd made. To my knowledge, such an editorial appendage to a critic's review was an historic first.

Rich took it upon himself to make a statement exceedingly

painful to me. He claimed that the role of Felix Turner, the lover who dies from AIDS in my play, and who worked as a reporter for the *Times*, was a fictional creation. No one bothered to check with me or with the Public Theater. Felix Turner had been my lover. When I immediately asked for space to rebut Rich's misinformation, it was refused me.

Rich threw a couple of great quotes into his review, I guess to hedge his bets. And Joseph Papp is that rare producer who is also a courageous promoter. He read us Rich's review immediately after the opening night's performance. And he vowed that he would keep the play running. And he kept his promise. To this day, *The Normal Heart* holds the record of being the longest-running play at his Public Theater.

Did *The Normal Heart* change the world? Of course not. But it did accomplish more than a little something here and there. It has been produced all over America and all over the world, including such unlikely places as South Africa, Russia, and Poland (and Poland is a land where there is such homophobia that gay people often commit suicide). In Lafayette, Louisiana, a town where they beat up gay people in the streets, the play was done by an amateur group, in a run that was extended twice and then repeated a year later; local straights joined the few local gays who were out of the closet to form an AIDS service organization. And, in Baton Rouge, the local drama critic came out of the closet in his review.

And I'd estimate a few hundred thousand people have seen what I wanted them to see—including two men actually kissing each other and in love and caring for each other and one of them dying in the other's arms. Human beings, just like those watching them.

And I did shame *The New York Times*. Though I still bitch at them continuously, their AIDS coverage is now better than it was.

And Joe Papp and Joe Papp's lawyers joined with me in offering on a stage the dramatic argument: AIDS was originally allowed to grow and grow and grow because the Mayor of New York is a closeted homosexual so terrified of being uncovered that he would rather allow an epidemic. This argument has now

entered the general discourse on the history of AIDS. And all
future historians will have no choice but to take note. I'm proud
of that. I'm proud that I've been able to help gays realize that
we who are proud do not have to be victimized by one of our
own who is ashamed. Yes, plays can help change history. If you
can keep the damn things running.

Going after a Mayor is one thing. Going after a First Family
is evidently quite another. It looks like the world will not see
Just Say No as it has seen *The Normal Heart*. Even my mother
thinks *Just Say No* was a flop because the *Times* review was so
hateful. It doesn't occur to her to ask: why did Mel Gussow
scream at me so much? As with *Four Friends*, the producer did
not have the resources to surmount a wretched *Times* review
and he closed the show.

Gussow accused *Just Say No* of being in the worst possible
taste. Is it bad taste to let a country be destroyed by a plague?
Is it bad taste for a Mayor to sell out his city? Is it bad taste for
a mother and father to hypocritically sell their son and their gay
friends down the river? Gussow, and others, didn't like it that
my characters lampooned real people. I don't like it that those
real people—and their actions and their attitudes and their secrets, their politesse—are killing me and mine. And I have a
moral right to present my case. It's bad taste that the critic for
New York's most important newspaper doesn't even try to understand my message, or convey it to his readers. Just because
my truth is light-years away from Mel Gussow's truth, that doesn't
make my truth in bad taste.

I have seen nothing but bad taste in the last nine years since
AIDS came into my life. On the part of this city, on the part of
this state, on the part of the federal government, on the part of
not just the *Times* but every major publication and network. Why
is it bad taste for me to point it out? To point out the venal and
crass hypocrisy that became the hallmark of the Reagan years
—and looks to be continuing during these years in the Bush—
seems to me not to be bad taste at all, but a way of maintaining
some sort of spiritual health. And the gay audiences who saw
Just Say No know exactly what I meant and mean. And, God

bless them, they were able to laugh. Perhaps it takes being pushed almost over the edge day after day for nine years to make you see a certain kind of truth.

But gay truths are different from straight truths. And most of the straight world does not wish to hear gay truths. Because, as all truth should, it often contains hurts enough for everyone.

But the trendy heterosexual world of politesse is stronger than we are.

And we are all dying for it.

CHARACTERS

EUSTACIA VYE

FOPPY SCHWARTZ

TRUDI TUNICK

GILBERT PERCH

JUNIOR

MAYOR

HERMAN HARROD

MRS. POTENTATE

Setting: The town house of FOPPY SCHWARTZ *in Georgetown, the capital city of the country of New Columbia.*

Time: The last weeks of Daddy's reign.

ORIGINAL
PRODUCTION

Just Say No was presented for a limited run from October 4 through November 6, 1988, at the WPA Theatre in New York City. It was produced by Kyle Renick, WPA's Artistic Director.

Cast

EUSTACIA VYE .... Tonya Pinkins

FOPPY SCHWARTZ .... David Margulies

TRUDI TUNICK .... Julie White

GILBERT PERCH .... Keith Reddin

JUNIOR .... Richard Topol

MAYOR .... Joseph Ragno

HERMAN HARROD .... Richard Riehle

MRS. POTENTATE .... Kathleen Chalfant

Director .... David Esbjornson
Scenery .... Edward T. Gianfrancesco
Lighting .... Craig Evans
Costumes .... David C. Woolard
Sound .... Aural Fixation
Production Stage Manager .... Paul Mills Holmes

PROLOGUE

(EUSTACIA VYE, *a black woman, comes before the audience.*)

EUSTACIA Listen my children, and you shall hear
How we came to be screwed so drear
By Mommy and Daddy, who make all the rules,
And then live by other ones—making us fools.
Yet some of us have survived the worst.
We got out alive, although we are cursed
For letting them flimflam us yet once again,
And again and again and again and again.
Someday we'll learn, that's this woman's plea.
So I tell you this story to help us all see
How we tried to fight, though given the shaft,
By their mob of the powerful, brutal, and daft.
A trivial comedy, Oscar once said,
But for serious people, before we are dead.

ACT ONE

Scene: The town house of FOPPY SCHWARTZ *in Georgetown, the capital of New Columbia. It's a house of highly ornate taste. The main living area (ground floor) contains a sofa and some chairs and tables and a built-in bookcase or breakfront with a large selection of movie videotapes. A TV set with VCR are downstage so the screen cannot be seen. On one wall is a big mirror for* FOPPY's *preening. The place is peppered everywhere with paintings and photographs of the rich and famous. Behind one big painting is a wall safe. Behind another is a reel-to-reel tape recorder. One area has a large regal chair and table with many phones, one of which is red. A master panel of switches is on the wall to control all the phones.*

On the ground floor are the following: the doorway to the Jean Genet bedroom; a grand staircase to the

second floor; the door to the kitchen and
EUSTACIA's *quarters; the front door to the outside*
world; and the doorway to the Oscar Wilde
bedroom. Up the staircase, on the second floor, are
the door to the Marcel Proust bedroom and the door
to FOPPY's *master bedroom. There is a small*
balcony that juts out above and over the front door.
Under this balcony, hardly seen, is a door to the
basement.

(Note: If a two-tiered set is not feasible, it is possible
that all rooms be on one level. It is also conceivable
that the presentation of the play be thought of in
nonrealistic terms.)

At rise, FOPPY SCHWARTZ, *in a handsome*
dressing gown and lounging pajamas, comes down
the stairway, talking on a portable phone. He goes
to his table to begin holding forth on several
additional phones. He talks on two at once, then
another one will ring, then another. Sometimes he'll
answer, sometimes not, as per his whim. When
someone more important calls in, he gets rid of the
caller of lesser importance. If a phone rings and he
does not wish to interrupt his call, he simply picks
up the ringing phone and hangs it back up again.
The table is littered with the day's newspapers, all
turned to the society and gossip columns. Several
elaborately wrapped gifts await his inspection on the
sofa.

FOPPY   Cynthia, of course a woman can have a best male
friend just as a man can have a best male friend. But a
woman cannot have a best woman friend because a best
woman friend will do her in. Whereas I won't. Stay away
from Carolina. She is evil. *(Picking up a ringing phone)*
Momentito, cara. Carolina, I am just telling Cynthia you

are evil. Yes, you are. Helene came all the way from Paris just to be seen in that hideous gown. You did not have to seat her next to me. *(Hangs up on Carolina, goes back to Cynthia, while a third phone rings, which he picks up and hangs up again to stop the ringing.)* Calvin got married? A fool and his mister are soon parted. *(Picking up another phone. To Cynthia:)* Scusi, ancora. Chesty, you smelled most peculiar last night at Nan's. Had you not time to bathe? Cynthia, *adios muchacha. (Hangs up on Cynthia.)* And return those shoes immediately. You are too old to parade your painted puckered tired toes. And buy your earrings even huger. To shroud your unfortunately gigantic lobes. Yes, Foppy is always in the know—of those things really worth knowing. Which are not so many as many think. *(Picking up a receiver that's been lying there all along)* Who is this? Marella, I must talk to Chesty, whom I like better today. *Ciao, bella*, kiss *tutti Venezia* for Fopp. *(Kisses her, hangs up; another phone rings.)* My precious Pat! Chesty, *domani, domani. (Hangs up on Chesty.)* I loathe that stupid moron who claims someone as divine as you could be his wife; a civilized society does not identify its sufferers with tattoos! Yes, I had to go with *her*. Yes, Mrs. Potentate needs her taste in all areas supported. Yes, I am her jockstrap. Yes, am I not the flower behind the drone. *Auf wiedersehn, shatzi. (Hangs up on Pat.)*

EUSTACIA *(Entering to serve him more coffee) Café, mon plus grand juive?*

FOPPY *Merci, ma petite noir. (Picking up another ringing phone)* Not again? Perry, Angelo, Way, Rock, that dreadful candelabra person, and Roy—well, we don't miss Roy. Who was it this time? It was only a question of time. Surrounded by so much ballet beauty. *(Into another ringing phone:) Aspetta?* Darling Suzy, have you heard? Robert has gone to dance in the sky. *(Into other phone that has been off the hook the whole time:)* Who is this? *Dica? Dica?* Oh, Mica! *(The red phone rings. He talks into all receivers at once.)* My dears, she is calling! *(He hangs up on all of them, then crosses to the red phone, putting it on speakerphone, after turning off the wall panel controlling the ringing of the other phones.)* My Royal Highness, what is this about your firing Uncle Donny? Foppy is delighted. Caligula taught us that disloyalty must be flogged to death.

MRS. POTENTATE'S VOICE   My Foppiness, we must speak in the utmost of confidence.

FOPPY   Your bitch is my command.

MRS. POTENTATE'S VOICE   Herman Harrod and his bimbo, Trudi Tunick, have disappeared. Poof!

FOPPY   Poof! Then we must have a joyful celebration luncheon at the Palace!

MRS. POTENTATE'S VOICE   They had an all-night sex orgy in some downtown sleazepit.

FOPPY   Too disgusting.

MRS. POTENTATE'S VOICE   Along with a big bunch of her bimby broad slut friends.

FOPPY   Too too disgusting.

MRS. POTENTATE'S VOICE   Some of Daddy's closest . . . associates were there. And someone filmed it. Someone made a home movie of it.

FOPPY   My Princess of Baker Street, how did you discover such drastic dish?

MRS. POTENTATE'S VOICE   Foppy, this is serious. I must locate that movie before it goes into general release. If you find out anything at all about anything at all, call Mommy. *(She hangs up.)*

EUSTACIA   The ideals that made our country of New Columbia great are now more than ever turned to ordure. *(To audience)* That's shit.

FOPPY   They have been a good mommy and daddy.

EUSTACIA   To you, white man.

(He begins to open and try on and model in front of a mirror various items from the assortment of gift boxes. She helps him.)

EUSTACIA   I was taught we get the government we deserve. All we had to do if we didn't like it is speak up. There are 23,011 lobbyists in this town. There are 12,612 journalists. There are 80,000 trade reps. It is impossible to speak up to 115,623 people.

FOPPY   Write your Chamberperson. *(Reading card, throwing it away)*

EUSTACIA   I wrote my Chamberperson. So did half a million other folk last year. Both Chambers sent 920 million back. That is 3,836,142 letters each working day. That is $144 million postage.

FOPPY   You are discovering democracy's flaw.

EUSTACIA   That Rifle Association sent three million telegrams in one day. They clogged up the Chamber switchboard so no one could call out.

FOPPY   That is why Daddy is against gun control.

EUSTACIA   His popularity was slipping. Getting shot was the best thing he ever did.

FOPPY   *(Trying on a robe, reading card)* Jackie! *(Admiring himself)* First you are young, then you are middle-aged, then you are old, then you are wonderful.

EUSTACIA   "Good evening, Ms. Wah Wah—may I call you Bah Bah? Thank you for allowing me to commit my memoirs to TV."

FOPPY   Eustacia, I have told you, never never talk to the media, not even in pretend. In Georgetown, pretend is the same thing as reality. (*Another gift, another card—he tears it into shreds.*)

EUSTACIA   But magazines pay big bucks for sexy titbits from all them hookers who screw with preachers and Potentate-in-Chief candidates.

FOPPY   You will never be a *Cosmo* girl and neither will I.

EUSTACIA   It is not for want of trying. I bet Bah Bah Wah Wah would offer me ten thousand dollars.

FOPPY   I'd strangle you for talking so cheaply.

EUSTACIA   "White Jew Georgetown Faggot Strangles Loyal Schvartzah for Talking Cheap." The Department of Drugs and Diseases spends . . .

FOPPY   Will you stop your numbers!

EUSTACIA   You think you're not a number? Daddy put an idiot in charge of Drugs and Diseases. If his IQ were any lower, you'd have to water him.

FOPPY   He gave Herman Harrod a generous contribution to Daddy's reelection. It is the way of the world.

EUSTACIA   I could retire on what I'm learning in this house about the way of the world. (*The doorbell rings.*) You get it. (*She goes back into the kitchen.*)

(FOPPY *opens the front door.* TRUDI TUNICK *stands there. She is lovely and nubile, and wears a hotel doorman's overcoat.*)

FOPPY   *(Preventing her entrance)* Who are you and what are you doing here and why must it be now?

TRUDI   Please. Someone very important is meeting me here. We never fly in the same cab.

FOPPY   I cannot allow you entry on such scanty information.

TRUDI   He said you're a gentleman.

FOPPY   How does he know?

TRUDI   Although I've never had much success with men, I suppose it's got to be different with gentlemen. He says this is a safe house.

FOPPY   Safe from what?

TRUDI   From him! He's on one of his hungry tempestuous rages. He's never satisfied.

FOPPY   I cannot bear to hear these acts. Whose are they?

TRUDI   Mine. His, too, of course. Herman says we're a great team. Like Anthony and Cleopatra.

FOPPY   Herman?

TRUDI   Oh, sorry. My name is Trudi Tunick, I am Herman Harrod's mistress and . . .

FOPPY   Come in, my Little Red Riding Hood. Why is Herman Harrod coming here when he knows Mrs. Potentate and I are best friends to his wife and therefore I must loathe him and you?

TRUDI   Herman wants you to help sell our sex tape to his wife. With Mrs. Potentate's help.

FOPPY   Tapes as in videotapes? As one would make oneself?

TRUDI   Oh, you make them, too? Isn't it great how anyone can make them? It's not like the old days when we
had to schlepp around such heavy equipment.

FOPPY   Tell me about your sex tape.

TRUDI   Now you can use itty lamps and bitty mikes and
don't the Japanese have the most clever little things?

FOPPY   Tell me about your sex tape.

TRUDI   And none of the actors have to be union members. If we did, I'd have my Screen Actors Guild card
by now.

FOPPY   Tell me about your sex tape.

TRUDI   I hope nothing's happened to him.

FOPPY   Describe your tape.

TRUDI   I wanted to be an actress so much.

FOPPY   My Debra Winger, describe your tape.

TRUDI   Tapes of people having sex.

FOPPY   Who doing what to whom?

TRUDI   Can't we wait for Herman?

FOPPY   My Meryl Streep, how many doing how much?

TRUDI   Herman wants to tell you himself.

FOPPY   What acts performed by which actors, Madonna?

TRUDI   Okay. Me and my girls having sex with Herman
and others.

FOPPY   Others who?

TRUDI   Others very important.

FOPPY   How important?

TRUDI   High-up important.

FOPPY   How high-up important? My English is being destroyed.

TRUDI   Very high.

FOPPY   The highest?

TRUDI   No. Herman says Daddy can't get it up.

FOPPY   That is classified information. How high up?

TRUDI   Have you heard the latest? Daddy's library just burned down. Both books were completely destroyed. Including the one he was almost finished coloring.

FOPPY   Who high up?

TRUDI   Herman says you can convince Mrs. P. to get Herman's wife to unfreeze his assets. Don't ever get married in California.

FOPPY   I won't. Pretty please. Who how high up?

TRUDI   (*Holding the newspaper*) You do crossword puzzles?

FOPPY   I do not do crossword puzzles!

TRUDI   What's the plural of moose?

FOPPY   (*Picking up a ringing phone*) Mistuh Schwartz, he dead. (*He hangs phone up, then removes it from cradle.*) Recite the entire cast of characters.

TRUDI   Don't tell Herman I told you, but they include: at least two elected Chamberpersons; at least three of Daddy's cabinet; at least four of Daddy's personal staff; at least five prominent businessmen listed on the Big Board; at least six . . .

FOPPY   Are we beating around the bush?

TRUDI   Oh, no, he's taken. He's had a mistress even longer than I've been with Herman. I can't give any more away for free.

FOPPY   How much do you have left?

*(She takes off her raincoat. She is wearing only an
S&M wardrobe—garter belts, hip boots, black
leather zippered this and that.)*

FOPPY   Evidently quite a bit. *(Admiring an item of her wardrobe)* Oh, this is nice.

TRUDI   Capitol Hill S&M. They have them for men, too.

EUSTACIA   *(Entering from kitchen with toilet plunger,
Drano, and wearing rubber gloves)* Old saying: He who lies
down with dogs gets fleas.

FOPPY   Be quiet. We are rooting out the truth.

EUSTACIA   I am cleaning out the toilet. *(She goes into
FOPPY's bedroom.)*

FOPPY   Where is the tape?

TRUDI   Never mind. I know where it is.

FOPPY   You can tell me.

TRUDI   I've been his mistress for twelve years. When he
had his first stroke, I moved into the hospital room next
door and looked after him while his wife went to all her
parties with you and Mrs. Potentate.

FOPPY   Where is it?

RUDI   Herman says I'll finally have enough money to
say "Get lost!" to everybody if I play my tape right. It
was his idea to make the movie. I'm not that smart.
That's why I am where I am, which is nowhere, in love
with a big bazooka who has trouble keeping promises.
Herman is one mighty promiser.

*(EUSTACIA comes out of FOPPY's bedroom and
heads back downstairs.)*

FOPPY And one of Daddy's oldest, closest, nearest, dearest, and most trusted friends. Herman is quite correct in believing Mommy would enjoy a private screening. Where is it?

TRUDI *(To* EUSTACIA*)* Who are you?

EUSTACIA What does it look like I am? A Nubian princess down on her luck. *(She goes into kitchen.)*

TRUDI In all eight years, Daddy didn't give Herman anything—not a cabinet post or being an ambassador or postmaster or head of a commission or anything. After all the money Herman collected for Daddy from all their friends in Vegas! Herman put it in a washing machine in one of those nice sunny places we go on vacation and then he gives it back all nice and clean to Daddy. But Daddy hasn't given anything back to Herman. Herman is one pissed-off Herman.

FOPPY Why is this pent-up vengeance suddenly surfacing now?

TRUDI Daddy only has a few more weeks in office.

FOPPY Herman only has a few more hours on earth.

TRUDI I know secrets that could bring down governments. I never seem to fall for great lookers with uncomplicated sex lives. The more fucked up everything is, the more Trudi Tunick gets involved.

FOPPY How much is Herman expecting to make?

TRUDI A million from Bob Guccione for the tape and a million from Hugh Hefner for my autobiography and a million from Larry Flynt for my body. I'd rather be in *Vogue*. Herman says you know everybody in *Vogue*. Mr. Schwartz . . .

FOPPY Yes, my dear?

TRUDI   I'm very frightened.

FOPPY   Why is that? Tell Mr. Schwartz.

TRUDI   I'm afraid.

FOPPY   Tell Uncle Foppy.

TRUDI   Marilyn Monroe murdered because she slept with Jack and Bobby and she knew too much. Dorothy Kilgallen murdered because she knew who killed Jack and she knew too much. Daddy elected Potentate-in-Chief because of MCA, and Jules Stein was from Chicago, Al Capone was his friend, you know what happens in Chicago. And JFK murdered by the Mob and Lee Harvey Oswald tied into the Mob, and Herman the connection between the Mob and Daddy. And Sidney and Paul and Nevada, you know what happens in Nevada. And one of Bill Casey's business associates was Mob, and Paul represented the Teamsters, don't forget the trucks, you can't make a move without the trucks. And Sidney's friend who worked for Jules lent Paul a fortune to buy casinos. And Howard Baker was on the board of MCA. And an important witness was murdered when Ray Donovan was under criminal investigation. And Jimmy Hoffa and Sam Giancana both murdered and Judith Exner slept with both JFK and Sam. And Leonore, whose husband owns the *Racing Form* and is Sidney's best friend and whose first two husbands were a casino operator and a bootlegger, is Mrs. Potentate's best friend. And all the people in Daddy's Koffee Klatch, Herman and Holmes and Walter and Joe and Earle and William, you know what happens when you drink too much coffee. And Mrs. Potentate started the Koffee Klatch. And Bill Casey died so suddenly—did *you* see his X rays? And all these people are Daddy's best friends! Oh, it's all connected, can't you see it's all connected, the entire network of every-

thing in this entire world, and you want to know why
I'm frightened, I know too much!, I don't know what
to do with it!, I don't know what to do period!, that's
why I'm frightened!

FOPPY   You're very special. And certainly clothed in
mystery.

TRUDI   Herman says the greatest mystery is how Daddy
got elected not only twice but once.

   (The doorbell rings.)

TRUDI   *(Starting for door)* That must be Herman.

FOPPY   *(Restraining her)* What if it isn't Herman? My dear,
trust Uncle Foppy, I must secrete you for a moment.
(He pulls her toward the door to Genet.) Now this is known
as the Jean Genet Suite and he was a very famous
Frenchman. I think you will recognize most of the outré
accoutrements of furbishment. Promise to stay hidden
until I and only I sound the All Clear.

TRUDI   I have always trusted in the kindness of
strangers.

FOPPY   You have been in error.

   *(TRUDI goes into Genet. The doorbell rings again.
   FOPPY rushes upstairs.)*

FOPPY   Eustacia, could you answer that?

   (EUSTACIA comes in to answer it.)

FOPPY   If Mrs. P. calls, I'll ring her directly after I pee.
(He goes into his suite.)

   (EUSTACIA opens the door. GILBERT PERCH

runs in. He is good-looking, a ditzy innocent, mid-thirties. He carries a small airline-type bag.)

GILBERT   *(Looking all around)* Are there any strange men?

EUSTACIA   All men are strange.

GILBERT   He's after me again.

EUSTACIA   Tell momma.

GILBERT   You are not my mother.

EUSTACIA   No shit.

GILBERT   My mother is divine.

EUSTACIA   So am I.

GILBERT   My mother is a sainted angel.

EUSTACIA   You got me there. I was only attempting to comfort you metaphorically.

GILBERT   My mother and I are just like that. *(He holds up both hands with the first two fingers crossed.)*

EUSTACIA   Gilbert, it's unhealthy for you to worship her so excessively.

GILBERT   You remember me? I'm that memorable?

EUSTACIA   Yes. *(Calling out)* Mr. Foppy!

FOPPY'S VOICE   Yes!

EUSTACIA   *(Calling)* That sissy-scaredy cat whose pants you could never get into? He's back.

(FOPPY comes out of his room, wearing another robe. EUSTACIA goes into the kitchen.)

FOPPY   Gilbert Perch! What are you doing here? *(He comes running down the stairs.)* I thought you were happily married to that pig.

GILBERT He is after me, after my body, after my brains, after my life, I can't take it anymore, he is driving me nuts, he says he loves me, he says he hates me, he says he's going to eviscerate me, he says he's going to pay me off with contracts and send me to the Coast, he says he's going to encase me in cement . . .

FOPPY Darling boy, it's so good to see you again. You've kept in shape. *(Feeling his arms and chest)* Sort of. The Mayor still has difficulty sustaining anything . . . permanent? He is too old to be so choosy. And ugly. He's much too ugly. And mean. He's dreadfully mean.

GILBERT I never want to see that choosy, ugly, mean old pig again!

FOPPY It does not sound like Cathy and Heathcliff.

(FOPPY *takes* GILBERT *to sit on the sofa, where he proceeds to make passes at him.)*

FOPPY Come, let us sit down and remember old times.

GILBERT You taught me how to overcome everything except fear.

FOPPY That is something you are born with, like impeccable taste.

GILBERT Nevertheless I'm still scared shitless.

FOPPY My fragile petunia, tell me what has happened since last you were in my arms.

GILBERT I was never in your arms!

FOPPY Alas. I could never understand why you chose him over me.

GILBERT Because he's Mayor of our largest northeastern city!

FOPPY   The aphrodisiac of power. Were you just manip-
ulating his . . . power? You could have chosen someone
who was . . . younger.

GILBERT   Younger? *(Pulling a large Rolodex out of his bag
and flipping through cards)* Major-league athletes? Olym-
pic gold medalists?

FOPPY   A little older.

GILBERT   A little older. Stars of weekly TV series?

FOPPY   A little older.

GILBERT   Older. *(Twirling his Rolodex)* Politicians elected
to high office? Stars of major motion pictures?

FOPPY   A little older.

GILBERT   Cary Grant is dead. *(He rips up the Rolodex card.)*

FOPPY   Tell me what happened.

GILBERT   You introduced us and he looked deep into
my eyes and said, "I want to spend the rest of my life
in your arms," and he took me to Appleberg and found
me a rent-controlled apartment and . . . I moved to Appleberg to become famous! I had the most famous lover
in the city! He got me a job in his Department of Sex
and Germs. Just to be near him. "You won't have to do
a thing, just come when I whistle," and he came every
Wednesday night, we ordered in, I can't cook. . . . He
told the world he loved Donny M., and then he said
Donny M. was a pig, and then Donny M. killed himself.
He told the world he loved Stanley F., and then Stanley
F. got indicted and went to prison. He told the world
he loved Bessie, but he wouldn't marry her either. And
then Mario B. got indicted, and then Donny T. started
saying nasty things, and then Geoffrey L. turned into
a stoolie, and then the latest polls showed less than 30
percent want him reelected . . .

(EUSTACIA *comes in with black satin sheets and crosses the stage.* FOPPY *jumps up.*)

EUSTACIA   If at first you don't succeed.

FOPPY   Must you always barge in unannounced! What am I paying you for?

(*She has climbed the stairs and goes into Marcel Proust.*)

EUSTACIA   Three hundred years of slavery.

GILBERT   (*The minute she's gone*) . . . and then he came every other Wednesday, and then he came one Wednesday a month, and then he came every other month, and then he stopped . . . paying my rent, and then in my job at Sex and Germs I learned all about the epidemic and I told him and he said, "Shut up, you gonif twit, it's a secret, haven't I taught you anything about secrets," and then a huge Italian man with a big, big gun came and gave me money and told me to keep my mouth shut and get out of town fast, don't even pack, or the ripple of destruction and the swirl of death would drown me in the river. And then the gay leaders discovered all about us, and came after me to blab the truth, they are ceaseless in their tenacious fixation to destroy him for destroying them, but they're coming after me, I'm caught in the middle, so all of this—all all all of this!—has brought me back to you, you are so good at social etiquette, can my love ever return him to the innocence of our bliss before he murders me?, he's coming after me, I know too much and he knows I know too much and he knows what I know could . . . He's running for a fourth term!

(*The red phone starts ringing.* FOPPY *jumps up, causing* GILBERT *to fall on the floor.*)

FOPPY *(Answering the phone)* Benevolent Regina, I must ask your indulgence while I clear the hall.

> *(He lays the phone down and escorts* GILBERT *to the stairway.)*

FOPPY Go up to my queen-sized bed to rest. . . .

GILBERT I knew I'd be safe with you. I promise I'll be good.

FOPPY That's good. Perhaps now that you're on the market again . . .

GILBERT You never told me he'd treat me like shit.

FOPPY He treats everyone like shit.

> (GILBERT *goes into* FOPPY's *room, closes the door.* FOPPY, *fanning himself, patting his heart, which now flutters with hope that* GILBERT *might now be his, picks up the phone.)*

FOPPY *Ritorna vincitor!*

MRS. POTENTATE'S VOICE Foppy, my body has needs.

FOPPY Your body has what? Now that you are about to be out of office, you are returning to your former life? Is that wise?

MRS. POTENTATE'S VOICE I don't know what you're talking about. You don't remember a thing about my early life except that it was blissful. *(Threatening)* Do you, dear?

FOPPY What becomes a legend most? I have something to tell you. . . .

MRS. POTENTATE'S VOICE One of my young lawyers is meeting me at your house. Is he there waiting and panting with impatience?

FOPPY No, my Supreme Sovereign, but I shall see that all is in readiness. What is this one's name?

MRS. POTENTATE'S VOICE You know I can never remember.

FOPPY Well, which law firm is he with?

MRS. POTENTATE'S VOICE One of those liberal ones we hate. Full of Jews.

FOPPY The true spirit of Bitburg. *(Locating a notebook)* Is it Ira Pecker of Paul Weiss Rifkind?

MRS. POTENTATE'S VOICE No.

FOPPY Is it Pisher Slotnick at Phillips Nizer Benjamin and Krim?

MRS. POTENTATE'S VOICE No.

FOPPY Is it Sammy Sugarman at Schweitzer Schwartz Shagan Shafran Sheps Subotsky Stolts Sheib Schecter Saperstein Sadow Sachs and Schlem? If it isn't, then perhaps you should not embrace the law.

MRS. POTENTATE'S VOICE Oh, all Jews sound alike.

FOPPY Recent events in Israel have changed so many minds.

MRS. POTENTATE'S VOICE Oh, my Foppirina, why do I perform these dangerous acts?

FOPPY Oh, My Challenger, How High the Moon! Now listen . . .

MRS. POTENTATE'S VOICE I think I remember what he looks like. Well, I'll recognize him with his clothes off. *(Her phone needs money.)*

FOPPY   My Sylvia Porter, why are you calling from a pay phone? Do as Foppy instructs you: extract any silver coin from your Gucci bag and drop it into any round hole it fits at the top. The woman has been in power too long.

MRS. POTENTATE'S VOICE   I'll be right over. Uncle Ed's reading Daddy his pornography report. No more dirty magazines in 7-Elevens.

FOPPY   The country will turn celibate overnight. Now, *senta*!

MRS. POTENTATE'S VOICE   *(Yelling over louder phone noises)* Have you found out anything yet about the tape?

FOPPY   I am trying to tell you . . . !

   (Dial tone is heard; she's been cut off.)

FOPPY   I must always remember this is not an Age of Reason. If this were the Court of Louis XIV, I would be the Duc de St. Simon. It is not and I am Foppy Schwartz.

   (The doorbell rings again.)

EUSTACIA'S VOICE   *(Calling from Proust)* You got it?

FOPPY   I got it.

   (He opens it and in comes running, perhaps leaping, and wearing only a raincoat, JUNIOR, a young man in his early twenties.)

FOPPY   First Son!

JUNIOR   I have a terrible problem!

FOPPY   It would be uncharitable to think that you alone were spared.

JUNIOR   Uncle Foppy, you've always been the only one I can turn to.

FOPPY   Secret floodgates are opening, gushing only in my direction.

JUNIOR   Pop has discovered.

FOPPY   It was bound to reach his hearing aid.

JUNIOR   His eyes. He saw me. I've never seen him so angry.

(JUNIOR *takes off his raincoat; he's wearing only a bath towel.*)

FOPPY   Does no one in this town wear clothes?

JUNIOR   *(He practices a few ballet steps in front of the mirror.)* I'm never going back. I'm making the leap. I'm going to Appleberg to find a man! I'm going to Appleberg to come out! I'm going to Appleberg to be a ballet dancer!

FOPPY   That'll do it, all right. Dance! Dance! Dancers start doing it at birth.

JUNIOR   So I started doing it at sixteen. I'm a late bloomer.

FOPPY   But you don't have the bud of a Bruhn, the stem of a Serge, the petals of a Peter. All you'll have is the stigma of a sissy.

JUNIOR   I have the elevation of the son of the Potentate-in-Chief.

FOPPY   They laughed Margaret Truman off the stage.

JUNIOR   I'm not a singer, I'm a dancer.

FOPPY   What will your mother say? Does she know? Does she know I know? There are numerous ballet dancers who are heterosexual men, although I can't think of any at the moment.

(EUSTACIA *comes down the stairs.*)

EUSTACIA   The CIA just bought more drugs from Noriega. Hi, Junior.

JUNIOR   Hi, Eustacia.

EUSTACIA   Tell your Daddy, since he took office the number of employees fighting illicit drug traffic decreased by 19,609.

JUNIOR   I told him. It doesn't do any good.

EUSTACIA   Tell your Ma, my sister on welfare's fourth-oldest son is dealing 20,000 bucks a week. It's real hard for her to Just Say No.

JUNIOR   You tell her.

EUSTACIA   Are you afraid of her?

JUNIOR   I love my mother.

EUSTACIA   Not another one. "Just Say No" has done for addiction what "Have a Nice Day" did for clinical depression. (*She goes into the kitchen.*)

JUNIOR   Which is my room? I'm moving in with you.

FOPPY   Oh, no, no. No, you're not. No.

JUNIOR   You always let me have overnights.

FOPPY   Tell me your story quickly. Give me the *Reader's Digest* version.

JUNIOR   I'm in love.

FOPPY   Give me the *Vanity Fair* version.

JUNIOR   I'm in love with both of them.

FOPPY Give me the *National Enquirer* version.

JUNIOR I'm in love with both my Secret Service men.

FOPPY Two of them? We are not Mormons.

JUNIOR The three of us were taking a shower in the Calvin Coolidge bathtub. They're not allowed to be separated in their devotion to my safety, they can't even take their guns off. . . . And we were all naked and soaped up and Daddy suddenly yanked back the curtain. "Well, Junior, what have we here?" he said, his cheeks full of that blush that everyone thinks is makeup when he's on TV and is.

FOPPY We must not frown on the necessity for a few personal vanities. Harry Truman wore a corset to tuck in his tummy.

JUNIOR Harry Truman didn't dye his hair.

FOPPY Continue your tale in a tub.

JUNIOR Randy snapped to attention. "Yes, Sir! Secret Service Man Randolph Pigeon of Huntington, Indiana, at your service, Sir!" and his you know . . .

FOPPY Guns in the shower?

JUNIOR . . . hard as a rod firmly flapping against the pulsating force of the shower spray. "Yes, Sir! Secret Service Man Dutch Gulliver of Tampico, Illinois, reporting for duty, Sir!" . . .

FOPPY The heartland of America . . .

JUNIOR . . . and his you-know . . .

FOPPY Tushie?

JUNIOR . . . ready, round and beautiful like a perfect pumpkin. Everything was beautiful, Foppy.

FOPPY You practice such behavior in these days of plague and death?

JUNIOR We swore on their guns not to exchange bodily fluids.

FOPPY But what happened to their guns?

JUNIOR They've both been reassigned to Lebanon. Foppy, it isn't right.

FOPPY Right! Right! Right! is Jesse Helms and Pat Robertson and your father. We have not lived in an age of Right and Beauty since Ancient Greece.

JUNIOR After Gull and Randy were taken away, Daddy picked up one of my ballet shoes and slapped me back and forth all over, up and down, I was still naked, and he screamed at me, "I whose Supreme Tribunal your mother and I have packed with justices to make you null and void," slash slash slash, "I whose Court System the Shyster General, first your Uncle William and then your Uncle Ed, and I have packed with Enforcers who know the words to 'My Way,' " slash slash slash, "I the Potentate-in-Chief of this great country of New Columbia have a little schmuck" slash slash slash "fairy ballet dancer son who sucks pee-pee."

FOPPY Such a nursery expression, pee-pee. Oh, the God of Jerry Falwell is cruel and merciless and unforgiving. Jimmy Swaggart did it with a hooker, but it was a female hooker.

(EUSTACIA *comes in from the kitchen with milk and cookies for* JUNIOR.)

EUSTACIA Why does Oral Roberts use that Christian name? Oh, well, my mother said never cry over spilt gism.

FOPPY   (*To* EUSTACIA, *confidentially*) Someone's mother will be here shortly. Prepare her suite!

EUSTACIA   We been here before. We know what to do.

FOPPY   We've been here one at a time. We've never been here (*Counting quickly*) four at once.

(EUSTACIA *goes back into kitchen.*)

FOPPY   (*Comforting* JUNIOR *in his arms*) I have always looked upon you as my son. But you must void my manse for the nonce.

JUNIOR   I can't go home again!

FOPPY   To his many other inadequacies, your wretched father must now be charged with child abuse.

JUNIOR   Daddy's a dick.

FOPPY   How has he won the love and affection of so many millions and for so long?

JUNIOR   Beats the shit out of me.

FOPPY   So you have said. Tomorrow. Come back to Tara tomorrow.

JUNIOR   Foppy, you were the first person I told I was gay. You told me I wasn't sick and to keep my mouth shut. Everything would be all right when I grew up. Well, I'm grown up. I want to open my mouth. I keep wanting to come out of the closet and you keep pushing me back in. As a public personality, I have a responsibility to my people. Our people! I want to be a contender!

FOPPY   My young Marlon Brando, your father does not like us. We must learn to wag our tongues from the inside.

JUNIOR   But all you do is go to parties with Ma's Dragon Ladies.

FOPPY   I am privy to much useful information. . . .

JUNIOR   But what do you do with it?

FOPPY   I . . . I . . . I advise your mother.

JUNIOR   To do what?

FOPPY   She looks best in red. . . .

JUNIOR   Doesn't she know you're gay?

FOPPY   We do not discuss it!

JUNIOR   Why not?

FOPPY   Why not, why not, youth wants to know? Because Mommy and Daddy are symbolic representatives of over 200 million people who look on us as freaks. Because what one does in the privacy of one's own home is nobody's business.

JUNIOR   But if we get laid it's rampant horrid promiscuity and if they get laid it's cause for celebration. If they're going to hate and kill us for doing what they do, too, what everybody does, then of course it's our business. You deny your true feelings.

FOPPY   Better than that she deny me all her Palace parties. One makes choices.

JUNIOR   The Supreme Tribunal makes its choice today. I'll bet we're going to be declared null, void, and illegal.

FOPPY   Only in Georgia. Maybe.

JUNIOR   And in twenty-five other states where we're a felony. We could be locked up for twenty years. I'll blackmail him. I'll tell the world about me. I am going to Appleberg to dance. With Robert!

FOPPY   You can't go to Appleberg to dance with Robert. Robert has just died.

JUNIOR   Oh, no! *(They hug each other.)* It's getting worse and worse and it's my own father's fault. How dare he! And you! With all you know, what are you doing? Help me, Foppy!

FOPPY   I know nothing. That I can tell you.

JUNIOR   When Uncle Rock was in Paris they wouldn't call him back.

FOPPY   He had made too many bad movies with Jane Wyman. Your mother told me she spoke to him every day.

JUNIOR   Not after they found out what was wrong with him. When you asked her to help get your friend that experimental treatment . . .

FOPPY   She didn't do it?! My beloved Bernie. . . . She didn't keep her promise?

JUNIOR   Foppy, you've got to help!

FOPPY   Your father was a cheerleader in college.

JUNIOR   A cheerleader?

FOPPY   With pompoms. When he was your age, he, too, was a momma's boy and a sissy.

JUNIOR   I am *not* a sissy! Pop?

FOPPY   In his early starlet days, he would emerge from the ocean at Santa Monica looking like an Adonis. He was always posing, exposing his then-beautiful chest. He was very popular. Among certain sets.

JUNIOR   Pop?

FOPPY   A little diddle now and then. One had a career to father.

JUNIOR   Pop?

FOPPY   Everybody did it. Cary Grant and Randolph Scott
and Tyrone Power and Errol Flynn. Well, Errol would
do it with anything that moved. It was a different world
then. Occasional transgressions did not require bomb-
ing Libya.

JUNIOR   So why does he hate us?

FOPPY   There is more. You are too young to remember
the Saturday Night Massacre.

JUNIOR   Pop went on a rampage with a gun?

FOPPY   When he was Prince of Orange. It was discovered
that a number of his closest staff were our brothers.
There was an unfortunate sex orgy at a cabin in the
woods. Some of them were men who were married.
One of them was a famous athlete who now desires to
be the Potentate himself. Drew Pearson of the *Georgetown Post* blabbed innuendo to the world. "It's an ill-
ness," your wretched father exclaimed, as he fired them
one and all. "They're sick, they're sick, they're sick!"

JUNIOR   What else? I must know everything. Come on!
It's time I knew all the facts of life.

FOPPY   In for a penny, in for a pound.

JUNIOR   I knew you knew more!

FOPPY   (*Very confidentially*) Your father had Hollywood's
largest collection of pornography.

JUNIOR   Old Howdy Doody! Are you sure that isn't gossip . . . ?

FOPPY   Gossip! Gossip! Gossip is life! And death. Be
careful with this knowledge, lest your mother be cor-
nered into silencing her own son.

JUNIOR   What do you know about her?

FOPPY   In for a pound, in for a fiver. There once was a
man named Benny Thau. No, I cannot. We have known
each other too long. I adore her. She adores me. Why,
we are so close, we know each other's very
thoughts. . . . *(The red phone rings.* FOPPY *collapses to the
floor.)* Never underestimate the power of a Queen. *(Answering)* What do you want!

MRS. POTENTATE'S VOICE   Procrastinators die!

FOPPY   *(Looking around to see if his house is bugged)* On
what evidence!

MRS. POTENTATE'S VOICE   Is he there yet?

FOPPY   My Lady Macbeth, what is this surprise package
I hear is being unwrapped today at the Supreme Tribunal?

JUNIOR   Way to go, Fopp!

MRS. POTENTATE'S VOICE   It has happened. The vote
was five to four. Tough break.

FOPPY   But you had indicated . . . I had so hoped.

MRS. POTENTATE'S VOICE   Daddy tried his best. One
of the justices was on the fence. But he fell off. Accidentally.

FOPPY   Accidentally?

MRS. POTENTATE'S VOICE   Be careful. Friends are one
thing; politics another. History is what we make it. You
are now illegal.

   *(*FOPPY *hangs up on her.)*

FOPPY   What have I just hung up on? What have I just
disconnected?

JUNIOR   Are you beginning to get motivated?

FOPPY   I may have some valuable information at my . . .
your . . . our disposal. . . .

JUNIOR   Uncle Foppy, you know everything! What is it?

EUSTACIA   *(Sticking her head out of the kitchen)* Need I
inform you of our unfolding saga. *(Goes back in the
kitchen.)*

FOPPY   *(Pushes* JUNIOR.*)* Go into Oscar Wilde. He was
accustomed to trouble. Although he did not survive it
. . . he fought back! "Yes, I am a dreamer," he said.
"For a dreamer is one who can only find his way by
moonlight, and his punishment is that he sees the dawn
before the rest of the world."

JUNIOR   Then I can stay? *(Throwing his arms around him
in gratitude)*

FOPPY   Until we die at dawn together.

JUNIOR   I'll practice my dancing. I've got to get in shape.

FOPPY   *(Getting him into Oscar Wilde)* Shape! What happened to symmetry and grace? Life was meant to have
grace. But she drove over a cliff. *(He starts up the stairs
to his bedroom.)* It is a far far better world I go to. . . . It
is time for me to change into basic black. Herman Harrod, you are forcing me to have my rendezvous with
destiny. I'm ready for my close-up, Mr. DeMille. *(He
goes into his bedroom.)*

> *(* EUSTACIA *enters with an armful of sheets and
> towels. At the same moment,* TRUDI *comes out of
> Jean Genet.)*

TRUDI   That's an awful room.

EUSTACIA   You're telling me. Who are you and what
are you doing in this house?

TRUDI   Does Mr. Schwartz trust you?

EUSTACIA   Like a sister.

TRUDI   I've come to sell top-secret information.

EUSTACIA   You know how? (TRUDI *nods.*) What's the secret?

TRUDI   Until you find the highest bidder, just say no.

EUSTACIA   My sister in bondage, embrace one willing to share all her knowledge in an effort to find the highest bidder.

TRUDI   (*Uncertain what she means*) Thank you, but I've already used all the girls I needed.

EUSTACIA   But you haven't even heard my story. My story is better than their story.

TRUDI   Maybe your story added to my story . . .

EUSTACIA   Would make one hell of an issue. I was born into a family of . . . no, I guess that's not so riveting. When I was thirteen, I lost my . . . no, no one's interested in poor white trash. It's not so easy to tell your story as I thought. You know, my story isn't really about me. Except to indicate in the broad cosmic sense that we women of New Columbia are in one big stinking mess.

TRUDI   What is it about?

EUSTACIA   Them.

TRUDI   Which them?

EUSTACIA   Which them you want? This house has been witness to every major them in recent modern history. You know how Nelson Rockefeller croaked stuck in a woman not his wife? (*Nodding to a bedroom*) He got stuck in there first. You know about Marilyn and Bobby? Right in there.

TRUDI   I was on Marilyn's bed!

EUSTACIA   Ike and his WAC. Lyndon grabbed a lot
of ass. JFK and Judy. JFK and Marilyn. JFK and
Emily. And Sally. And Wenonah. And Ellie. And Patsy.
And . . .

TRUDI   I identify so with Marilyn.

EUSTACIA   Did you know that the CIA went into her
house right after and cleared out everything? No evidence was left. Not a shard.

TRUDI   I know. I know.

EUSTACIA   Dorothy Kilgallen same thing. Dead and
nothing to show for it.

TRUDI   I know. Herman produced a show with Dorothy's husband. I took acting lessons. Mr. Strasberg told
me, "I see in you many of the qualities of the young
Marilyn." But then Herman and I sort of got caught up
in politics.

EUSTACIA   Poor Jack. He may have screwed more than
his share, but he didn't screw the country like some
others we know who are also screwing more than their
share.

TRUDI   Could I ask you a favor? Could I give you something very important for you to lock up in a safe safe?

EUSTACIA   How safe?

TRUDI   Real safe. (*She takes the tape out from under her coat.*)
It's the only copy.

EUSTACIA   I could buy the old plantation.

TRUDI   You could buy the whole Confederacy.

EUSTACIA   Our downtrodden asses could be the ruling
classes. Why are you giving this to me? (*She gives it back
to her.*)

TRUDI I'm scared to death it will fall into the hands of men who don't understand. *(She gives it back to her.)*

EUSTACIA I understand. *(She doesn't. Gives it back to her.)* I thought you just said no until the highest bidder?

TRUDI I'm afraid the highest bidder might be God. *(Giving it back to her)*

EUSTACIA *(Taking it)* Oh, I was trained to take up the white man's burden. *(Hides the tape on her person. They embrace each other.)* We women got nine lives and we've walked through eight of them, but that doesn't mean they can call us pussy.

(The doorbell rings, then rings again. FOPPY rushes out from his bedroom, in an extravagant robe of many blacks. He is appalled to see TRUDI.)

FOPPY Here only minutes and broken your promise. Return to incarceration! *(TRUDI rushes back into Genet.)* Eustacia, ready Mrs. Potentate's rose hip tea.

(EUSTACIA runs to the kitchen as the doorbell continues to ring and ring.)

JUNIOR *(Sticking his head out of Oscar Wilde) and* EUSTACIA Should I answer the door?

FOPPY No!

(EUSTACIA returns to the kitchen. FOPPY rushes toward the front door, stopping to check himself in the mirror first. Then he opens the door. The MAYOR tries to come in. FOPPY does his best to prevent him but loses. The MAYOR carries a suitcase and a bag from the Gap. As he talks, he walks around investigating, looking outside through

the drapery, peeking in the kitchen, the bathroom,
FOPPY heading him off as he starts for Oscar
Wilde, Jean Genet . . .)

MAYOR   God, they make you beg in this town. They
make you grovel. They make you eat shit. So I got a
few municipal problems. I am not technically responsible. It's nothing can't be fixed with federal graft. All I
want's a few billion. That's bubkus. I got spilkis. Is he
here? My dick followed him here. The Big Appleberg
has got to have his little cherry. I've come to kill him.
Imagine making me testify! It's all the fault of the drug
dealers. We got to murder them *before* they get in the
country. You got anything to eat? I only diet in Appleberg. I'm here to pig out. Where is he? I know he's here!
How'm I doing?

(*He tries to open Jean Genet.* FOPPY *restrains*
him.)

FOPPY   He's not in there!

MAYOR   Who's not in there! We better be alone.

FOPPY   We are all alone. It is the existential dilemma.
Who are you looking for?

MAYOR   No one. Is he here? My private dick followed
him to this neighborhood. But he lost him. I got to get
back to Grovel Hill. I got more bastards and pricks to
threaten. Fatso Kennedy. Dukakis the secret psycho.
Jesse the Hymie Hater. I got to gore Gore. Have I been
lured here under false lasciviousness? I'm not gay, you
know.

FOPPY   You are talking to Foppy.

MAYOR   I forgot.

FOPPY   If homosexuality could claim all those who dis-
claim it, it would be larger than the Catholic Church.

MAYOR   Franny Spellman warned me. Young morsels
are trouble. But he could handle them. I miss my old
friend, Franny. This new cardinal is a pain in the cas-
sock.

FOPPY   He's just like you. He hates everybody.

MAYOR   That's why we get along so well. (*He starts eating*
JUNIOR's *cookies.*) Milk is bad for me. (*He drinks the milk.*)
I'm intolerant.

FOPPY   You should have stayed with that adorable Gilbert Perch. He loved you.

MAYOR   If I ever see him again, I'll blow off his pecker.

FOPPY   You are in a state of denial.

MAYOR   State schmate. I'm the mayor. Nobody can
touch me. My people love me. The nastier I am, the
more they love me. That's the secret of running a big
city. Hate. How'm I doing? You sure he's not here? I
threatened all those bureaucrats and now I'm horny.
My streets are clean. I just got a lot of people like to
sleep outdoors. I got no disease. I got no epidemic. I
just got a lot of fairies. Nobody can see fairies. They flit
around invisible.

FOPPY   As Peter Pan warned, you must never not believe
in fairies.

MAYOR   Which one's my room?

FOPPY   You cannot stay in my house!

MAYOR   (*Checking out videos on the shelf*) Of course I can
stay in your house. I've stayed in your house since we
were kids together at Cherry Grove.

FOPPY   You were my first.

MAYOR   Mine, too.

FOPPY   And it was an unpleasant experience.

MAYOR   I'm not gay, you know.

FOPPY   Of course not, my J. Edgar Hoover.

MAYOR   It's ludicrous to think I'm gay. I am only speaking the truth as I know it. Don't you find you're happier and you do a better job by telling people exactly what you think?

FOPPY   But the truth is Appleberg stinks with scandal and corruption.

MAYOR   Are you trying to tell me I smell?

FOPPY   As a matter of fact, I am.

MAYOR   What's come over you?

FOPPY   You smell. Your politics smell. Your administration smells. Your subways smell. Your bridges are falling down. Stepping in your ocean is like swimming in an unflushed toilet.

MAYOR   Get over it.

FOPPY   To even open a restaurant now requires a bribe. What's come over me?

MAYOR   You don't want to open a restaurant. Very high rate of failure.

FOPPY   Why are you letting all your boys be devoured by this horrible plague without lifting a finger?

MAYOR   You should talk? What have you done with all your fancy shiksa friends? All you do is go out with helmet-headed Barbie dolls to fress. (*Takes a video from the bookcase.*)

FOPPY   Bite your tongue.

MAYOR   Tongue, nova, perch, quail, as long as it's cir-cumcised. God I'm hungry. The truth is it's the pushers and the junkies and the spics and the micks and the dago mobsters and the chinks. Who would have thought Chinese? I like their food. I got the best record of corruption of any major city. Any misdeeds commit-ted by former allies now in jail, out on bail, awaiting trial, I am not technically responsible. It's all pisher-dicka. Listen, I didn't come here to talk shop. I need a randy-dandy. *(He is heading upstairs with his bags.)*

FOPPY   A what?

MAYOR   A schtuck in the pupik. You found me Gilbert Perch. Find me someone else! Now! *(He goes into Marcel Proust.)*

FOPPY   I won't find you anyone else!

MAYOR   *(Opening door and yelling out)* I want a pupik! I want a randy-dandy. I'm not gay. I am not technically responsible. How'm I doing? *(He goes back into Proust and slams the door.)*

FOPPY   *(Running to his desk)* He denies everything like Kurt Waldheim. *(Consulting an address book)* Timmy is busy . . . Thadd's away . . . Thumper is with Claus von Bülow. I haven't been so nervous since Guy Burgess schtupped Dean Acheson and moved to Russia.

   (EUSTACIA enters.)

FOPPY   The Mayor's in *her* room!

EUSTACIA   What! After all he's done to all your people and mine.

FOPPY   We have to get him out of here!

EUSTACIA   *You* have to get him out of here!

FOPPY   I have to get him out of here! Maybe Junior's
right. Something's got to be done. Someone's got to do
something. Where is that tape? Why am I pimping for
all these pimps? What have they ever done for me? Have
you removed all my photographs of framed European
royalty from Marcel Proust? The First Lady doesn't like
to be reminded that she isn't Queen for Life.

EUSTACIA   How many times the First Lady come here
to . . .

FOPPY   (*Covering her mouth*) No no no, don't use the F
word!

EUSTACIA   If that's what they're doing to all of us, why
not?

FOPPY   You never get in trouble in Georgetown for lying.
You only get in trouble for telling the truth.

EUSTACIA   Whose truth?

FOPPY   What's happening to me? Eustacia, I'm tired of
being a hag fag. Is this a way to live out one's life? I
think it's time to change the world.

EUSTACIA   What would you do with the tape if you had
it?

FOPPY   I was going to give it to the First Lady.

EUSTACIA   Wrong answer. After all she's done to all
your people and mine.

FOPPY   You're right! You're right. What am I saying?
What am I doing?

EUSTACIA   You tell me. You're supposed to be the smart
one.

FOPPY   If I am not for myself, who is for me?

EUSTACIA   Keep talking.

FOPPY   And if I am only for myself, what am I?

EUSTACIA   A selfish pig.

FOPPY   You are correct.

EUSTACIA   You are a mensch.

FOPPY   And if not now, when?

EUSTACIA   I love it.

FOPPY   And if not me, who?

EUSTACIA   Us! *(Hands him the tape.)*

FOPPY   We must look at it.

(They rush to the VCR. FOPPY puts in the tape.)

FOPPY   *(As they look at it)* Our Trudi tells the truth. One, two elected Chamberpersons. One, two, three of Daddy's Cabinet. One, two, three, four of Daddy's personal staff. . . . I think we've struck . . .

FOPPY *and* EUSTACIA   Deep doo-doo.

EUSTACIA   There's no time for more now. Put it in the safe safe. *(She takes the tape out of the VCR.)*

(He rushes to the wall, pulls back a painting, and reveals a safe. He starts twiddling the dial, with EUSTACIA looking over his shoulder. He can't remember the combination.)

FOPPY   What's the combination?

EUSTACIA   I was hoping to learn it from you.

FOPPY   It's on the horse's ass.

(He runs to a small statue of a horse on a table.

GILBERT *comes out of* FOPPY'*s bedroom, just as*
JUNIOR, *wearing nothing but undershorts, comes*
out of Oscar Wilde. FOPPY *sticks the tape in his*
robe pocket, which EUSTACIA *notes.)*

GILBERT   Fop, do you . . . Oh. Hello.

JUNIOR   *(Looking up)* Hello.

FOPPY   Good-bye.

EUSTACIA   I'm not wanted on this voyage. I'll be in the
slave gallery if you need me. *(Goes back into kitchen.)*

GILBERT   *(Starting down)* Say, isn't your face familiar?

FOPPY   No. *(Taking off his robe and throwing it on* JUNIOR*)*
Clothe thy seductiveness!

JUNIOR   I'm Junior. *(Offering his hand)*

GILBERT   I knew it. I can't tell you my name yet because
I'm hiding from a powerful pig, but I'm very happy to
meet you . . . *(Taking his hand)*

FOPPY   No no no no!

GILBERT   . . . even though I hate your father.

FOPPY   Not as much as his father hates you.

JUNIOR   So do I.

GILBERT   You do?!

(They're still holding hands. FOPPY *tries to break*
them apart, which he can't. He's also trying to
either get the tape out of JUNIOR'*s robe pocket, or*
get the robe off JUNIOR*.)*

FOPPY   No no no no no NO! *(To* JUNIOR*)* You have been
incarcerated in mansions and palaces too long to make

wise decisions. *(To GILBERT)* You have been in bondage to a monster too long to play such a dangerous game. *(To JUNIOR)* This is not the moment to make such a public statement for gay rights. *(To no one)* I am going to be electrocuted before teatime.

JUNIOR   I'm very happy to meet you, too. I have led a sheltered life. But that's all going to change.

GILBERT   I'll be happy to show you the ropes.

FOPPY   Ropes.

GILBERT   I have a great Rolodex.

FOPPY   I am going to be sent for dinner to Qaddafi.

GILBERT   Can I have your number?

JUNIOR   I'm staying here at present.

GILBERT   So am I! Which room is yours?

FOPPY   Mine. The one with the little chair and the electric wires connected to the tubes of gas.

JUNIOR   Why don't you come in and we can get to know each other better?

FOPPY   Please. I shall be cut into small pieces and processed into the horse meat consumed at roadside burger stands from coast to coast.

JUNIOR   You sound so strong and intelligent and in control.

GILBERT   I'm sorry, Foppy, but Junior is more famous. I feel we have a future together.

FOPPY   *(Proclaimed like Lady Bracknell's "A handbag!") A future?!* *(As they go toward and into Oscar Wilde)* Make your bed and go and lie in it. No, make your bed and only lie on it. No, don't lie. Think of higher things. No,

don't think of higher things. Out of sight, out of mind.
I am out of mind. (JUNIOR *opens the door and tosses*
FOPPY *back his robe, which he puts on.*) I am an aging man
trying to do good too late in life and I have only one
life to give and I'm about to give it. His schtuck in the
pupik is randy-dandying it in the house that awaits his
mother. We who are about to die pollute you.

(*The* MAYOR *comes out of Proust, holding his
videotape.*)

MAYOR   Yuck. This is some disgusting slime. Do heteros
really do all that to each other?

FOPPY   You tell me. You're not gay.

MAYOR   Did you find me anybody yet? He better be safe.
We don't have any AIDS in Appleberg. We don't have
any homos in Appleberg. They all live out of state. (*He
puts the videotape back with the others.*) The sheets are black
satin. I got to have different sheets. Static electricity is
too . . . exciting. Change the sheets! (*Going into the
kitchen*) Eustacia, here comes your favorite hozer! Piggy
piggy piggy!

FOPPY   (*Screaming out in frustration*) Aiiiiii!

TRUDI   (*Rushing out*) Mr. Schwartz, you are so tense.
Trudi knows how to relieve tense. Have you got a fever?
(*She removes his robe, massages him.*)

FOPPY   I've got a fever. I've got a fever.

TRUDI   Are you having a breakdown?

FOPPY   I'm having a breakdown.

TRUDI   (*She sits him down on the sofa.*) I've had lots of
them. I belonged to a support therapy group in Malibu
called the Malibu Maligned Malingerers although you

don't have to be from Malibu. But you do have to be maligned. My therapist said you have to fall completely apart before the pieces fit back together.

FOPPY I'm falling completely apart.

(She is massaging him and he is relaxing. The doorbell rings.)

TRUDI I'll get it.

(She runs to answer the door. HERMAN HARROD, in full leather regalia, including whip, stomps in, slamming the door. He ignores FOPPY and goes for TRUDI. She hands him FOPPY's robe and HERMAN grabs it and puts it on. They begin fighting as if they've never stopped.)

HERMAN The hotel impounded my clothes because you didn't pay the bill!

TRUDI How could I pay the bill?!

HERMAN *(To FOPPY)* You tell your friend Mrs. Potentate that if she doesn't order her best friend my wife to cosign some checks . . . *(To both of them)* I'll blackmail her! *(To TRUDI)* You got the tape someplace safe? *(She nods. He rubs his hands together with gleeful greed.)* Give it to me. When I die you'll be rich.

TRUDI I don't want you to die. I just want to be rich.

HERMAN *(Snorting some coke)* Now my snotty wife will be forced into releasing my money.

TRUDI *(Meaning the coke)* Don't you ever get enough?!

HERMAN Never! *I'm* the rich one. It's my money! Macy's, Bloomingdale's, Harrods. The Big Three at Yalta. I married her poor! When I die, she'll probably bury me

in a two-buck coffin. She pays up or the entire world
will know about us. You and me, Trudi and Herman
and our orgy and sex scenes and whips and chains and
leather and thigh-high wading boots and rubber and
masks and the rack! . . .

(FOPPY *has been trying to get his hand into the
pocket of the robe* HERMAN's *now wearing, to get
the tape.*)

HERMAN   Get out of here, you pervert!

(HERMAN *comes after* FOPPY *with the whip.*
FOPPY *starts running up the stairs.* TRUDI *starts
talking to get* HERMAN's *attention back to her,
and he returns.* FOPPY *stays on the stairs,
listening to the conversation.*)

TRUDI   You said I could have a house of my own. You
said you would look after me forever. You said after I
did it with the Shyster General I could stop finding girls
for your White Palace friends. Aren't you tired of being
pimp to the Palace? You said you were Daddy's best
friend and you could get anything and after twelve years
all I've got is nothing but some dirty home movie and
my autobiography that isn't even written yet.

HERMAN   It's not my fault. I helped put that lousy actor
into office and what happens? He learns how to act. I
screened all his applicants for high office. I shaped his
policy. I chose his issues. I found him (*A snort each issue*)
anti-abortion, and the Lord's Prayer, and the Pledge of
Allegiance, and the holiness of the family, and the sin
of perverted faggots. I made the shidduch with Jerry
Falwell. I got Gary Hart into trouble. I got him millions
of bucks from Vegas. And what does Daddy give me?
Dickshit. You don't exile Herman Harrod from Disney-

land and get away with it. You got some girls we could call for a quickie?

> (He tries to get a hold of TRUDI and she continuously evades him.)

TRUDI Girls, girls! You're insatiable. It's just like Wall Street, pure greed. You said we could go back to kiss and cuddle. I'm not girls! I am a woman!

HERMAN How do you know we won't kiss and cuddle? Remember how we cuddled when I called Sam Giancana? And Albert Bonnano? What a turn-on!

TRUDI Men don't understand. Sex doesn't mean that much to most women. It's not exceptional. It's not.

HERMAN It is! It is! You don't appreciate how good you are at it. You always shovel shit all over your good qualities.

TRUDI It's hard finding girls who don't mind getting whomped by a strange man, even if on paper he's one of the richest men in New Columbia and best friend to the Potentate-in-Chief. A whip's a whip.

HERMAN I don't whomp hard.

TRUDI You do, too! Unless I harness your horsepower.

HERMAN Harness my horsepower!

TRUDI LaWanda said it's hard for her to make a hundred bucks a day, but at least when she's making three and a quarter an hour at Wendy's she knows she'll be alive when she goes home to get smacked by her husband.

HERMAN Call LaWanda.

TRUDI The Catholic Church has a lot to answer for, letting you in.

HERMAN   You leave the Church out of this. I'm real
generous to the Church. I got cardinals and archbishops
friends of mine. I got blessed by the Pope! *(Showing his
crucifix)* Every time we have one of our little sexy
scenes—oooh come here—I go to my own personal con-
fessor.

TRUDI   He must have cast-iron ears.

HERMAN   I was a Jew who became a Catholic and a
Democrat who became a Republican. I didn't know
when I was well off. One year I spent a million bucks
on hookers. My wife just doesn't understand me.

TRUDI   You're a very complicated person.

HERMAN   Don't you love me?

TRUDI   Any dream is better than no dream. I didn't
know you got Gary into trouble. She was a friend of
mine. I thought what we did in private was our business.

HERMAN   It is our business. Except when it's their business. Then it's big business.

TRUDI   It's dirty business. I'm scared. You can't just
blackmail Daddy and get away with it. They have all
kinds of secret weapons.

HERMAN   I have all kinds of secret weapons. Where's
the tape? *(His hands have found it in the pocket of* FOPPY's
robe he's wearing.) It's an omen! It's an Act of God. Thank
you, Jesus! *(He rushes to a phone, makes a call.)* Hello,
Huggy Buggy Bunny Boo. It's your husband, you nitwit.
Marvin Michaelson filed suit. Trudi Tunick wants $10
million palimony. Now will you sign some checks or
must she tell the world! No? Then how about this. We
filmed our latest S&M orgy with some of Mommy and
Daddy's closest chums. Put that in your braces and get
lockjaw.

(TRUDI *has managed to get the tape as* HERMAN *talks on the phone.* HERMAN *hangs up, rips off his robe, and starts chasing* TRUDI *around the room. She is running from him, and* FOPPY *is fanning himself, overcome with all the excitement.*)

TRUDI   You have that crazy look in your eyes.

HERMAN   Tell me how crazy.

TRUDI   Very crazy.

HERMAN   Ten million from the palimony and millions from the media and I want to be Ambassador to France!

TRUDI   I love Paris!

HERMAN   Paris was made for kiss and cuddle!

TRUDI   Be careful, Herman Harrod, you're going too far.

HERMAN   Pull me back, babe, don't let me go too far.

(*He falls on all fours and starts following her. She starts guiding him around with the whip. She sees* FOPPY *watching and whips the air that he should go away. He goes inside his bedroom, but keeps the door open and peeks out.* TRUDI *has been looking for a safe place to hide the tape; hastily she puts it on the shelf with all the others.*)

TRUDI   Tell me how important Trudi Tunick is in your life and forever.

HERMAN   You rule my world. You're master of all passion. Don't let me go too far.

FOPPY   You go too far.

HERMAN   Tell me anything you want!

TRUDI   I already told you a million times.

HERMAN   Tell me again.

TRUDI   I want you to take care of me forever.

HERMAN   Forever and ever.

(*He is on his back on the floor behind the sofa. She unzips her skirt and sits down . . . behind the sofa, too. A sudden sound of everything suddenly stopping and going silent.*)

TRUDI   Herman. Herman? Herman! (*Sounds of her slapping his face*) Mr. Schwartz!

(FOPPY *rushes down, pretending to just arrive.*)

FOPPY   Yes, my dear.

TRUDI   I . . .

FOPPY   Yes?

TRUDI   I . . . I . . .

FOPPY   Yes yes?

TRUDI   I can't . . . I can't . . . I can't get off!

(EUSTACIA *comes in with a tray with the necessities for tea.*)

EUSTACIA   Teatime. Time for tea. Rose hip tea and little finger sandwiches.

FOPPY   Not now with the hips and fingers!

EUSTACIA   There is a black limo pulling up outside *chez toi* and a woman wearing a bright red Adolfo fake Chanel suit is walking toward our hacienda and in just a minute the doorbell is going to . . .

(The doorbell rings. EUSTACIA *helps* FOPPY *get* TRUDI *and* HERMAN *upright.)*

TRUDI Why can't I get off?

EUSTACIA You have an iron in your fire.

(They start hauling TRUDI *and* HERMAN, *who is stuck in her, maneuvering them toward Jean Genet.)*

TRUDI Oh, Herman, you told me I don't have enough fuck-you money yet! How can I ever do it without you?

EUSTACIA So far you won't ever have to.

FOPPY Both of you—stop beating a dead horse.

TRUDI You're only supposed to say nice things about the dead!

FOPPY Being hung like a horse is saying something nice.

(The doorbell continues to ring. JUNIOR *sticks his head out of Oscar Wilde; he's wearing only a towel.)*

JUNIOR Anybody got any rubbers?

*(*EUSTACIA *quickly puts herself between* JUNIOR *and the couple.)*

GILBERT *(Also in towel, sticking his head out, too)* Anybody got any Trojans?

EUSTACIA This party's BYO.

JUNIOR Fourex lambskins?

GILBERT Ramses Kling-tite with Nonoxynol-9?

EUSTACIA   You gonna have to make do with spit, your hands, and restraint.

JUNIOR   Even generics?

EUSTACIA   We're running a whorehouse, kids, not a drugstore. *(She pushes them back into Oscar Wilde.)*

FOPPY   This is not a whorehouse!

MAYOR   *(Coming out of the kitchen)* Is that for me?

FOPPY   Let me inspect him first, in case he's a troll. *(Pushing him back into the kitchen; sounds of crash)*

> *(The pounding continues.* EUSTACIA *and* FOPPY *get* HERMAN *and* TRUDI *into Jean Genet.* FOPPY *grabs his robe, puts it on, checks himself in the mirror.* EUSTACIA *straightens up.)*

FOPPY   *(Motioning that he is ready)* Eustacia.

> *(*EUSTACIA *opens the front door.* MRS. POTENTATE *enters. She wears a huge hat and enormous sunglasses and carries a handbag.)*

FOPPY   *(Kissing her hand)* Mrs. Potentate, Proud Mommy, welcome once again to the House of Schwartz.

End of Act One

ACT TWO

(The action resumes immediately. FOPPY *is kissing*
MRS. POTENTATE'S *hand.* EUSTACIA *closes
the front door.)*

FOPPY   Mrs. Potentate, Proud Mommy, welcome once
again to the house of Schwartz.

MRS. POTENTATE   My tasteful one, I feel like a million
bucks. No, a billion.

FOPPY   Why not? As long as the budget is not balanced.

MRS. POTENTATE   Is he here?

FOPPY   He? You still cannot summon up a name?

MRS. POTENTATE   *(Removing her hat, sunglasses, and
gloves, and handing them to* EUSTACIA*)* He's still not
here? Who does he think he's screwing with? I haven't
got all day. It's not as if I was having a slam bam with
some bimbo in some uptown sleazepit fophouse.

FOPPY   But do you have time, my Lily of France?

MRS. POTENTATE   *(To* EUSTACIA*)* Bring me a glass of
cold water. With twelve aspirin.

EUSTACIA   Sounds like a heavy habit, Ma'am. *(She goes
into the kitchen.)*

FOPPY   With so much tape on your plate, my Wily Wedg-
wood, is it not best to return to service at the Palace?
How is there time for . . .

MRS. POTENTATE   A first lady always finds time. For
the really important things. That's what I get laid for.
Even as we talk, it's being taken care of. Fopp, it seems
ages since we dished. How are you? How do you feel?

FOPPY   Like the man who stokes the dank at Monte
Carlo. What's being taken care of?

MRS. POTENTATE   Carolina told me that you called her
evil.

FOPPY   Carolina? Georgia is evil. What is being taken
care of?

MRS. POTENTATE   Herman Harrod, the bimby slut, the
tape, the location, the co-conspirators, punishment.
That's what I have an SS for!

FOPPY   Even as we talk?

MRS. POTENTATE   Even as we talk. *(Flopping down on the
sofa and reclining)* God helps me, Fopp. My kingdom come!

FOPPY   A family that prays together stays together. I
must confront her. Next week. Next month. Next year.
How do I get her out of here? So I can live till next year.

MRS. POTENTATE   Why isn't he here yet?

FOPPY   My Miss Marple, how can you concentrate on so
many mysteries at one fell stoop?

MRS. POTENTATE   So what if I don't know his name? He doesn't have to have a name. It's not his name I want. Do you think I caught Alzheimer's that time I kissed Rita Hayworth?

FOPPY   To think that once I considered myself fortunate to be born rich, educated at the best schools, drilled by the best dentists, and so welcome and well traveled in the world of the rich and famous. I thought it all meaningful. *(To her)* Perhaps he is an Orthodox Jew and prefers to do it only after sundown.

MRS. POTENTATE   No one's as orthodox as all that.

FOPPY   Not yet, my Golda Meir. *(He crosses himself.)* You have heard about Robert?

MRS. POTENTATE   Sad. Sad. Oh, my Prince Charming of the Law . . . hurry hurry . . . my young Felix Frankfurter . . .

FOPPY   With each minute, the score grows and grows. More and more of our dear friends are dying. Robert; my dearest old love, Bernie, whom you helped so much. . . .

MRS. POTENTATE   *Not remembering Bernie at all)* Dearest Bernie. Sad. Sad. More than ever we must live life to the fullest every single minute. You must not dwell on a past full of lost Bernies.

FOPPY   Which of us has a past that's passed, my Nancy Reagan?

MRS. POTENTATE   Oh, Fopp, aren't I awful? *(She is dialing on her phone.)*

FOPPY   You are awful!

MRS. POTENTATE   KY 123 to KY 1. All this intrigue makes me even hungrier. I am ravenous. When it gets like this, I am insatiable. Darling, I'm at Uncle Foppy's.

(To FOPPY*)* Kiss kiss from Daddy. Yes, he knows you hate the faggot breath he walks on.

FOPPY   Kiss kiss back to Daddy, too.

MRS. POTENTATE   Not yet. We haven't found a thing about a thing. Don't get depressed. We'll just have to shoot you up again. If the media calls, just play dumb like you did so well with Iran. I'm still in there. No! Not in there! In there fighting for glorious New Columbia! *(Disconnecting)* He always thinks I'm still being such a naughty girl. I love it! I'm never so ravenous as when there's a good hot knotty steamy . . . *(She falls on the floor in ecstasy.)*

FOPPY   Will she never have her change of life? *(Helping her up off the floor and leading her upstairs)* All play and no work makes the sack a dull joy. Come—let us await fate in Marcel Proust. In remembrance of things past . . . *(Getting her into Marcel Proust and closing the door)* She would get laid during the Crucifixion.

MRS. POTENTATE   *(Coming out)* While I have you here. Junior is also missing. I found a note in his wastebasket.

FOPPY   You read his basket?

MRS. POTENTATE   It said, "I'm going out into the world to dance, you bitch." What do you think it means?

FOPPY   First Mother Mary's son, Jesus, also spoke in parables.

MRS. POTENTATE   Thank you! Come help me prepare me to meet my maker.

(She pulls him into Marcel Proust.)

MAYOR   *(Coming out of the kitchen)* So what did he look like? *(Seeing no one is there)* He must have been pretty ugly. *(Phoning)* Bessie, you is my woman now. It's time to get married. I'm running for reelection. We can pretend, just like the last times. Why not? You got caught what? Forty-four bucks worth of lipstick? You just found it in your pocket? Forty-four bucks worth of lipstick and you just found it in your pocket? What were you wearing? A truck! *(He hangs up.)*

(EUSTACIA *comes in with a glass of water and some aspirin. The* MAYOR *grabs the aspirin, puts them in his mouth; she prevents him from taking the water.)*

EUSTACIA Mr. Foppy says use his room temporarily.

MAYOR Why? Is nothing permanent in this joint?

EUSTACIA We got the exterminator.

MAYOR What you got?

EUSTACIA Rats. You should understand. *(She goes back into the kitchen.)*

MAYOR Forty-four bucks of makeup and I lose my beard. How am I going to get reelected? How long can I keep it up? A little longer. Only a little longer. *(Studying the movies)* On Golden Blonde. My Bare Lady. Ilse, She-Wolf of the SS. Yuck. Beverly Hills Copulator. *(He takes this one.)* This sounds out of state. Who else can I get? The Duchess of Windsor's dead.

(The MAYOR *comes back and takes another tape, the* tape, *which he sticks in his crotch.)*

MAYOR Movies are seven bucks.

(The MAYOR *sticks the first tape in the VCR and settles down to watch it.* EUSTACIA *comes out of the kitchen with more aspirin and goes up and knocks on Marcel Proust.* FOPPY *comes out.)*

EUSTACIA   I told him he had to stay in your room. (*She goes into Proust.*)

FOPPY   (*Rushing down to the* MAYOR) You must wait in your room. I sent away one ugly troll. But I've called one more. Be Prepared!

MAYOR   (*Removing the tape*) This is disgusting. I want something dirty and gay and juicy. Is this one any good? *Jules and Jim.*

FOPPY   No wonder the arts in Appleberg are not allowed to flourish. (*Helping the* MAYOR *to move upstairs*) Go up and play with yourself. My screen is larger. *Jules and Jim* will make you very envious.

MAYOR   I'm tired of playing with myself.

FOPPY   What good news! I must notify the *Appleberg Times.* Then take a bath. Take a douche. Take two. They're small.

MAYOR   I don't have to stay here, you know. There are plenty of places in this hick town to get my doodah diddled. I'll stay. (*He goes into* FOPPY'S *room.*)

(FOPPY *runs downstairs.* EUSTACIA *comes out of Proust and downstairs.*)

FOPPY   (*Knocking and opening the door to Jean Genet*) Oh, I see you're still engaged.

EUSTACIA   What are we planning to do since the plot got infinitely more complicated?

FOPPY   (*Running to the wall safe*) Unless you have trusted friends who don't ask questions at Frank Campbell, I must make calls.

EUSTACIA   This is no time for you to chat with any of your bitchy women.

FOPPY   This is precisely the time. Leave me alone to do so.

*(He opens the safe, takes out a secret little black
book. He slams the safe shut and rushes to a phone.
She follows him as he starts to phone.)*

FOPPY   Is the Chamberperson in? Eleazer Ben Schwartz.

*(EUSTACIA, now that she knows he is getting to
work seriously, gets up and heads into the kitchen.)*

FOPPY   *(To EUSTACIA)* Go unhelp unscrew her.

*(EUSTACIA goes into the kitchen and immediately
comes out wearing rubber gloves and carrying a
large can of Crisco. She goes right into Jean Genet.)*

FOPPY   *(Into phone)* I desperately need your help. You have
never heard me speak like this before. If I had the most
powerful instrument of blackmail known to modern
man, what would our people want? What do you mean,
who are our people? You are talking to Jack Lemmon in
The Apartment! *(Listens)* Hmmm. Hmmmm. Unh-hunh.
Would Daddy ever do that? No, of course not. He hates
the faggot breath we walk on. Would you help? Of course
not. You do, too. Return your key immediately! *(He slams
down the phone.)* I am a man possessed. I must overthrow
this wretched dynasty and Their Supreme Reprehensible
Hypocrisies, but I don't have the weapon for her destruction in my hand—my instrument for her doom.

*(We suddenly hear an enormously loud sound of
something going POP! . . .)*

FOPPY   Aaaaachhhh.

(. . . followed by an enormous sigh of relief from
TRUDI. *The doors to Oscar Wilde and* FOPPY's
bedroom open and their inhabitants— MRS.
POTENTATE, MAYOR, GILBERT, JUNIOR—
stand in their respective doorways.

FOPPY   It was nothing! It was one of those thousand
points of light. *(Each returns into his or her bedroom. To
audience:)* What does that mean?

(EUSTACIA *comes out of Jean Genet, followed by*
TRUDI.)

TRUDI   How many ways do you spell relief?!

MRS. POTENTATE   But I recognize that sound!

(MRS. POTENTATE *rushes out of Marcel Proust,
wearing a lingerie outfit à la Fredericks of Hollywood.
Her face is all creamed up.* EUSTACIA *pushes*
TRUDI *back into Jean Genet, going in with her.)*

FOPPY   I should think you would. My Helen of Troy, go
back! Continue creaming!

(But MRS. POTENTATE *comes down anyway.
She looks around as she rushes for a regular phone
and starts to dial.)*

FOPPY   Go back to Marcel Proust. In search of lost time.

MRS. POTENTATE   *(Into phone)* My Friend, is there any
sign of danger in today's chart? No, I don't plan to travel
over water. *(She hangs up.)* To walk on it perhaps.

FOPPY   My Forever Amber, you must prepare for it. You
are about to have it. And enjoy it. And celebrate it. But
you're really not quite ready. Your face is slimy. Your
hair is mangy. I can see your zit. You're a mess!

MRS. POTENTATE   Oh, dear. You really think so?

FOPPY   I do. And who taught you everything you know?

MRS. POTENTATE   You did.

FOPPY   I did. And may history forgive me. First Mother of Love, From Whom All Yessings Flow, go back to your Chambre D'Amour as we await the law.

(He has her back in Proust. No sooner does he start down, then she comes out again.)

MRS. POTENTATE   Foppy Schwartz, answer me directly! Is Junior a confirmed fairy?

FOPPY   Confirmed in the sense of accepted into the faith? Bar mitzvahed?

MRS. POTENTATE   Answer me!

FOPPY   As Tallulah Bankhead once said, "Well, darling, he's not sucked my cock."

(MRS. POTENTATE *goes back into Proust.*)

FOPPY   George, we're all doing our bit to make it a kinder, gentler nation.

(FOPPY *opens Genet.* TRUDI, EUSTACIA, *and* FOPPY *start schlepping* HERMAN *out.*)

TRUDI   I thought when you die you got lighter.

EUSTACIA   What are we going to do with him?

TRUDI   I want him buried with full military honors. I'll wear a beautiful black pillbox . . . *(She gets caught up in her fantasy, walks forward, dropping her part of* HERMAN, *who falls on the floor.)*

FOPPY   The basement. Temporarily.

EUSTACIA   Old trunks. Like in *Arsenic and Old Lace*.

FOPPY   Arsenic. Yes, I could try that.

TRUDI   Herman's used to old trunks. I locked him up in
them lots of times. Oh, Herman! How can I stand up
to your wife in a palimony suit? She's a very smart lady.
How can I sell a tape to the world? I couldn't even sell
Mary Kay Cosmetics. *(Some item of* HERMAN's *gets
stuck.)* Our love handcuffs!

FOPPY   My dear, so many years of such devotion to such
a horrid human gives you rights. You must stand up
for them and fight.

TRUDI   It's easy for you to say. You're a somebody.
Courts and lawyers and the media will believe you.

FOPPY   Let us fervently hope.

TRUDI   *(To* HERMAN*)* Between your wife and Mrs. Potentate, I am dead.

MRS. POTENTATE'S VOICE   Foppy!

FOPPY   Yes, my Bella Lugosi! Does the vampire never rest!

TRUDI   I know that voice! She's come after me already!
She's found us! Boy, she doesn't waste any time.

> (MRS. POTENTATE *comes out on the landing.*
> EUSTACIA *quickly covers* HERMAN *with a sheet
> and* TRUDI *hides by the stairs.* EUSTACIA
> *polishes the banister with her apron, to stand
> between* TRUDI *and* MRS. POTENTATE.*)

MRS.   POTENTATE   Are you telling me Junior just
hasn't quite found himself yet?

FOPPY   Am I telling you that? Yes! Why not?

MRS. POTENTATE It upsets Daddy to see him flapping around the White Palace.

FOPPY We, too, were flappers once.

MRS. POTENTATE I tried to explain to Junior that running a country is more important than watching a fairy dance *Swan Lake*.

FOPPY There are no fairies in *Swan Lake*.

MRS. POTENTATE There aren't?

FOPPY Swans. There are swans in *Swan Lake*.

MRS. POTENTATE (*Going back into Proust*) Then perhaps it's just a stage.

(JUNIOR *and* GILBERT, *both in bath towels, and very much in love, come out of Oscar Wilde.* EUSTACIA *pushes* TRUDI *into the kitchen.* FOPPY *runs back to the phone.*)

EUSTACIA You'll be buried, Herman. All we need is the dirt.

GILBERT I'm telling you, there isn't anyplace we can live safely. Who would let you live openly anywhere and particularly with me?

JUNIOR Boy, that bastard Mayor sure gave you psychic scars. I have a lot of work to do on you.

GILBERT You're willing to do a lot of work on me?

JUNIOR Of course.

GILBERT No one's ever said that to me before. Will it hurt?

FOPPY (*On phone*) Equal Fidelity Insurance. I wish to speak to your President. Tell him . . . tell him Butch Ramrod. R-A-M-R-O-D.

EUSTACIA That's my man. *(She goes into the kitchen.)*

FOPPY Big Dick, it's Butch. It's time to mobilize our members.

JUNIOR I wonder if Mom would lend us her decorator. Probably not.

FOPPY But you are one of the richest men in the world! Why can't you help insure us?

GILBERT Decorate what? Where? It's got to be some place safe from everyone after us.

JUNIOR We're going to live together like two men! In Appleberg!

GILBERT I can't live in Appleberg! What about Orange-burg?

FOPPY What do you mean, since when did I become such a radical fairy!

JUNIOR We must live in Appleberg!

FOPPY Since I started knowing twits like you, you twit! *(Disconnects. Makes another call.)*

JUNIOR It's the artistic capital of the world. Don't you want to grow as a creative person?

GILBERT I knew it would happen. Our first fight! Everybody famous is just alike. Having your way with me. Unresponsive to my genuine needs.

FOPPY First Secretary, Foppy Schwartz. Since your daughter is one of us . . . *(He is hung up on.)* I don't know who else to call. *(Thinks of someone.)* Yes, I do! *(Looks for the number.)* When you're in such a big and exclusive private club, you can always find another member.

JUNIOR I know what we can do. The first thing when we get to Appleberg we'll have couple's therapy.

GILBERT   Maybe we could live on the Island.

JUNIOR   No—we are going to live right out in the open!
If I can make one poor kid feel better because he loves
his best boyfriend, then I will have done some good.

FOPPY   Wolf Studios? Give me your big, bad boss, Barry.

GILBERT   You're such an inspiration. You give me so
much courage. Soon I'll be able to speak out. Just be
gentle.

JUNIOR   You're getting better already. See what love can
do?

FOPPY   I know that you have lost forty-seven friends.
Then you must understand. Understand what? That we
must do something. What must we do? You must make
a major motion picture at your major motion picture
studio. We must confront the Potentate! We must make
him attend to our growing emergency! Hello! Hello! You
will not be receiving the Rock Hudson Award for Ser-
vices to Your People! *(Hangs up. To* GILBERT *and* JU-
NIOR:*)* Did either of you by some remote impossible
one-in-a-trillion chance discover a sweet little videotape
in a robe pocket?

GILBERT   We've both been sort of busy.

JUNIOR   To watch movies. Are you all right, Uncle
Foppy? You seem distraught.

FOPPY   Your debut has presented many problems. Perhaps it fell on the floor. *(He goes into Oscar Wilde.)*

JUNIOR   You know they say a lousy dress rehearsal
means a hit.

FOPPY   *(Coming out of Oscar Wilde)* Don't give up your
day job. *(He is looking all around the living room.)*

JUNIOR   We've made our vows. We're going to live together as two men in love.

GILBERT   With you.

FOPPY   A menage à trois?

JUNIOR   *(To* GILBERT*)* Don't be a silly billy.

GILBERT   *(To* FOPPY*)* Don't be a silly billy.

FOPPY   My Damian and Pythias. My David and Jonathan.
My Simon and Garfunkle. Uncle Foppy would be so grate-
ful if you would go out and take in a movie! Now!

   *(They head back into Oscar Wilde, holding hands,
   dewey-eyed.)*

FOPPY   Not again!

JUNIOR   You can't keep kids from fucking 'cause it feels
so good! *(He breaks from* GILBERT *and runs over and hugs*
FOPPY*.)* Thank you for helping me find love. And for
becoming such a warrior. Foppy the Great!

   *(*JUNIOR *and* GILBERT *go into Oscar Wilde.)*

FOPPY   Foppy the Late.

TRUDI   *(Coming out of kitchen)* I really don't think I should
stay in this house any longer. You've been very hos-
pitable, but—I hate to say this to you—your house has
bad vibes.

   *(*HERMAN *falls out of the kitchen, covered in
   sheet.* MRS. POTENTATE *comes out of her room,
   looking ravishing, talking on a portable phone as she
   comes running down, modeling for* FOPPY*.*
   EUSTACIA *quickly covers* HERMAN, *and* TRUDI
   rushes back into Genet.)

MRS. POTENTATE   *(Into phone)* Yes, Mommy will be
home to dress you for tonight's performance. Yes, it's

a new costume. Yes, the Marine Band will play you in. Yes, there is a long, long, long red carpet. Yes, Sam Donaldson's on a long, long, long vacation. Yes, Mommy will ask Uncle Ed if he's been a bad boy. Now, stop worrying and go back to watching "General Hospital." Or play with your trains. Well, find something to do while I'm still in there. . . . No! No, listen to me: not in *there*! I've been a good girl since . . . I told you, I'm trying to save your . . .

EUSTACIA   Evil empire.

MRS. POTENTATE   No. We can't go. I haven't a thing to wear.

FOPPY   I'd lend you one of mine, but you haven't returned anything since 1982.

MRS. POTENTATE   *(Disconnecting)* Sometimes life is such a trial. No, I mustn't use that word. Oh, God, I need it. *(To* EUSTACIA*)* Darling, go to your place.

EUSTACIA   My place is to call Charlayne Hunter-Gault or Oprah Winfrey. *(She goes back into the kitchen.)*

MRS. POTENTATE   What's under that sheet?

FOPPY   The department store sent us the wrong order.

MRS. POTENTATE   Which department store?

FOPPY   Harrods.

MRS. POTENTATE   You ordered all the way from London?

FOPPY   All the way. And it's not returnable.

MRS. POTENTATE   *(Sitting down and pouring herself some tea)* I'm ready to explode! Can you see how passionate I feel?

FOPPY   Yes.

MRS. POTENTATE   Do you know what it's like to really
need it?

FOPPY   Yes.

MRS. POTENTATE   The only time he really comes to life
is when we stick him in front of the camera. Otherwise
we hide him. Do you have any idea how desperate it is?

FOPPY   Yes.

MRS. POTENTATE   The latest problem is he mixes up his
movies with real life. He plays with footballs in his bathtub and wakes up in the middle of the night to see if his
leg is still there. His leg! The hardest thing I've had to
deal with in over thirty years of marriage is his leg!

FOPPY   That is exceedingly desperate.

MRS. POTENTATE   Every time he passes a New Columbian flag he salutes it. Do you know how many New
Columbian flags there are in the White Palace?

FOPPY   (Calling off) Eustacia, how many New Columbian
flags are there in the White Palace?

EUSTACIA'S VOICE   (Calling back) Seven hundred and
twelve.

MRS. POTENTATE   I don't know why everyone thinks
this job is so much darn fun. Everyone thinks it's all free
dishes, mink coats, and retirement cottages in Orange-
burg. Foppy, they bought us the tiniest, mingiest house
in Bel Air. After all we did for all of them, they only
bought us two bedrooms. And Betsy Harrod hasn't been
any help in this mess with Herman. "Don't you dare yell
or threaten," she said to me, "I have $64 million. How
much do you have?" But I'm making the best of it! A cup
of tea makes you feel so brisk. (She starts upstairs again.)
Lady Bird planted her pansies on the highways. Eleanor
Roosevelt was a lesbian with bad teeth. Mamie was a

lush. Betty Ford was such a mess she opened her own cure. Roslynn was Attila the Hun. Pat Nixon pleaded a bad heart and she certainly had one. Who even remembers Bess Truman? All she was was just a wife and mother. I'm better than all of them. Mrs. Wilson ran the country, so can I! Why don't I get as good press as Jackie? I dress better and my husband is faithful.

(She goes into Marcel Proust and slams the door.)

FOPPY   I know Jackie! Jackie is a friend of mine! Mrs. Potentate, you are no Jackie! I wonder what it is like being friends with Barbara Bush?

(EUSTACIA and TRUDI rush out. TRUDI runs to the bookcase.)

TRUDI   Mr. Schwartz! The tape is gone!

FOPPY   I know, dear. How did you know?

TRUDI   I put it in the bookcase.

EUSTACIA   Where did you get it?

TRUDI   From Herman.

FOPPY   No one must leave the house until we find that tape.

(They all place their hands on top of each other, in a pact. The MAYOR comes out of FOPPY's room and heads toward Marcel Proust.)

FOPPY   Where are you going?!

(EUSTACIA covers HERMAN. TRUDI rushes back into Jean Genet.)

MAYOR   I need my jeans. You know I can't do it without my jeans!

FOPPY   (*Who's rushed up to cut off the* MAYOR) No, no, no, you can't go in there!

MAYOR   The exterminator's still here?

EUSTACIA   Yes.

FOPPY   And it takes a long time. Eustacia, get our beloved Mayor some more food.

EUSTACIA   He already ate everything we got!

FOPPY   Whip him up something!

> (EUSTACIA *goes into the kitchen. The* MAYOR *comes downstairs.* FOPPY *knocks on the door of Proust.*)

MAYOR   I'm not really into real whips. Although I'm getting closer.

FOPPY   My Tess of the D'Urbervilles. I am running out of things to call her. I need that suitcase and that sweet little bag from the Gap.

> (FOPPY *goes into Marcel Proust.* EUSTACIA *comes out of the kitchen carrying a tray on a stand; the tray is heaped with anything she could find. She starts feeding the* MAYOR *to keep his mind occupied.*)

EUSTACIA   Yummy yummy yummy. You want to tell me how come schools in your city are so shitty?

MAYOR   (*He eyes the covered body.*) Not me.

EUSTACIA   Buildings so falling down no one can learn?

MAYOR   When I decide to tell you, I'll tell you.

EUSTACIA   Don't you want my people educated? Seventy percent of our kids don't get through school.

MAYOR I can't argue with you because you're *wrong.* *(He starts to pull off the sheet.)* What's this sheet?

EUSTACIA Cover-Up. Fawn Hall for Wamsutta. How come you starve so many homeless?

MAYOR They're not hungry. They're demented. Look, if you feel guilty, see a priest. *(Eyeing the sheet again)* What kind of sheets on Foppy's bed?

EUSTACIA One hundred percent cotton. Picked by slaves. How come so many people on your payroll taking kickbacks? Crime and murder and manslaughter at new historic heights.

MAYOR You're very nosy. My people love me. They stand in line to picket me. I thought down South you people knew your place.

EUSTACIA *(Continuing to constantly feed him)* My people hate you. My people are going to kill you. There are more of my people than you think. You better not run for another term.

MAYOR Voodoo politics.

(FOPPY comes out of Proust with the suitcase and the Gap bag. He leaves them on the landing. He suddenly sits on the stairs, exhausted.)

FOPPY I am losing strength to be role model to 24 million people.

MAYOR Your Jesse keeps stirring up the schvartzahs, I got enough bigoted whites to get me reelected. I got a black police chief, they can't accuse me of racism. *(He's back looking at HERMAN's covered body.)*

EUSTACIA I hear everybody boos you now everyplace you go.

MAYOR   Boo, boo to you, too. *(Leaving the body)*

EUSTACIA   Eighty-five percent of women and ninety-two percent of babies with AIDS are people of color.

MAYOR   What kind of verkokte place is this?

FOPPY   Verkokte.

MAYOR   At least I shut them up in fancy welfare hotels.

EUSTACIA   You can't even build a skating rink!

(The MAYOR *comes back, heads straight toward her. She stands her ground.)*

EUSTACIA   You want all faggots and schvartzahs to die!

MAYOR   Don't forget the pimps and hookers.

(He heads back toward HERMAN's *body.* FOPPY *jumps up, rushes down, just as the* MAYOR *pulls the sheet off the body.)*

MAYOR   *(To* HERMAN*)* I thought so. *(To* FOPPY*)* You were right to hide him from me. He's not my type. Listen, there's big trouble in River City. I try never to be around when there's big trouble. I'm spending the night. *(He takes his suitcase and the Gap bag.)*

FOPPY   What am I going to do? There is no room in the inn!

MAYOR   That's your problem. You know when I plotz, I plotz.

MRS. POTENTATE'S VOICE   Foppy, can you come and look!

MAYOR   The exterminator's a woman?

EUSTACIA   What can I tell you you don't already know?

FOPPY I see why Sean Connery quit. *(He goes into Proust.)*

MAYOR Tawana, Billy Boggs, Robin Givens, all women are trouble. Go away and leave me alone.

EUSTACIA Beside every great man there is a woman. How you doin'? *(She goes into the kitchen.)*

MAYOR *(Phoning)* Bessie, I'll get one of my judges to squash the lipsticks. We can still pretend to get married and I'll get reelected and after you've shown your devotion to me you can go back to stealing again. What do you mean, you've been indicted by the chief DA, Rudolph Giuliani? What do you mean you're in love with a married convicted sewer contractor twenty-one years your junior? What do you mean you hired the judge's daughter to be your secretary? What do you mean so you could get his alimony lowered? You pooh-poohed with your secretary? You utz-putzed with your secretary who's the judge's daughter? Put Hiram on! Hiram, keep that about-to-be-convicted-again criminal quiet! What! The latest Gallup Poll shows 88 percent of my people want me to disappear? What? What tape? A friend of yours and Bessie's is on some sex tape? Bessie's going to squeal unless I get that tape? You'll both tell all about our life together unless I get that tape? Is everyone in Appleberg going mashuganah! *(He hangs up.)* No Bessie! No schtuck in the pupik! When will I learn: never trust old friends. They get indicted. How long can I keep it up? I was just looking at that tape! *(He starts running back upstairs. As he passes* HERMAN:*)* It's amazing guys your age think you can get paid for hustling. . . . Are all men expected to perform endlessly and forever? Who remembers old Appleberg mayors? Impellitieri. Lindsay. Abe Beame. Wagner and La Guardia had three terms. I got to have four terms. I got to get it up one more time. *(He goes with his suitcase and Gap bag into* FOPPY's *room.)*

(The stage is quiet for a minute. GILBERT *comes out of Oscar Wilde, still in towel.* TRUDI *comes out of Genet at the same time as* GILBERT.*)*

TRUDI　Who are you?!

GILBERT　Permit me to introduce myself. I don't think I can say my name out loud quite yet. Someone is still after me.

TRUDI　Someone is always after you.

GILBERT　My beloved mother has always taught me all the world needs is enlightenment. But I'm discovering enlighteners have nothing but trouble.

TRUDI　What do you have that's enlightening to sell?

GILBERT　I have secrets that could bring down administrations!

TRUDI　I have secrets that could bring down governments! Sounds like we could be a good team. Like Sean and Madonna. Like Woodward and Bernstein. I'll show you my secrets if you'll show me yours.

GILBERT　You first.

TRUDI　Do you know how to write an autobiography?

GILBERT　I once worked in the mailroom of William Morris.

TRUDI　You smell nice. Like you've just made love.

GILBERT　*(Blushing)* I have.

TRUDI　Did you kiss and cuddle?

GILBERT　Yeah.

TRUDI   Who with?

GILBERT   I can't tell you. You see, I'm running from an ex-lover who's high-up important.

TRUDI   Who how high-up important?

GILBERT   A choosy, ugly, powerful, mean old pig.

TRUDI   You mean the mayor of our largest northeastern city? Oh, God, we're both young, undressed, and on the run.

GILBERT   Precisely what have you got?

TRUDI   A sex tape of Herman Harrod and some of Daddy's staff and best friends in an S&M orgy.

GILBERT   Yikes. That smells pretty high. And just what we need. You see, I'm in love with Daddy's son.

TRUDI   You're not. Oh, congratulations!

GILBERT   Thanks.

TRUDI   I was kind of hoping . . . I find myself suddenly available. But I think that's just swell. . . .

GILBERT   With your tape . . .

TRUDI   But I don't have the tape. It got waylaid. It's here somewhere. . . .

GILBERT   When we find it, not only will we be allowed to live free in the eyes of the world, but we—all all all of us—could make enough money to live happily ever after.

   (EUSTACIA *enters.*)

EUSTACIA   Shhhhh. You'll disturb the rats.

GILBERT   Eustacia, is there another shower in the house? Junior seems afraid to take a shower with anybody.

EUSTACIA   Come on, you can use mine.

GILBERT   *(To* TRUDI*)* After I clean up, we can have our
first story conference.

   (They exit. TRUDI *uncovers* HERMAN.*)*

TRUDI   Herman, for a minute there, I didn't know what
I was going to do. Now I have hope again. I just don't
know what to do with you. You're still a problem. Don't
worry about me. I started over lots of times before. I
can do it again. I think. Good-bye, baby. I just wish you
could tell me about the tape!

   (She starts to go back into her room.)

HERMAN   Unnnhhhhh.

TRUDI   This house is a real trip.

HERMAN   Unnnnhhhh.

TRUDI   *(Going to him cautiously)* Herman? You're trying
to tell me something?

HERMAN   *(Moving hand)* Unnnhhhh.

TRUDI   You're trying to write me something?

HERMAN   Unnnnnhhhh.

TRUDI   Herman, you're still alive?

HERMAN   Unnnnnhhhhh.

   *(*TRUDI *rushes to* FOPPY'*s desk, gets a piece of
   paper and a pen, rushes back to him.)*

TRUDI   Write Trudi. *(As* HERMAN *laboriously writes, she
reads.)* "Tape . . ." Where is it, baby? Why am I asking you?
I had it last. But everything is worth nothing without the
tape. Where is it? I guess we're right back where I started.

(She is looking at herself in the mirror. An arm wearing a black glove suddenly reaches out, covers her mouth, and pulls her into Jean Genet.)

HERMAN Unnnhnnnhhh!!!

(JUNIOR comes out of Oscar Wilde, still in his bath towel. He takes huge ballet leaps around the room.)

JUNIOR I leap over the nunnery walls! I leap out of East Berlin! The land of the free! The home of the brave! Born free! . . . Oh, hi, Mr. Harrod. I didn't know you were here. Have you seen a cute young man in glasses?

HERMAN Unnnhnnnnhhhh!

JUNIOR Tough shit. I'm sorry you don't approve.

HERMAN Unh.

JUNIOR Well, he's the best thing that ever happened to me. You knew I was gay?

HERMAN Unnnh.

JUNIOR Well, I am, and I'm proud of it!

HERMAN Unh.

JUNIOR Are you all coked up again?

HERMAN Unnnnh.

JUNIOR You want some more?

HERMAN Unnnnhhh.

(JUNIOR finds coke and a spoon in HERMAN's pocket and gives him some more.)

JUNIOR Ma should just see you now.

HERMAN Unnnnnhhhhhh.

JUNIOR   Yeah, she can really be a pain in the ass.

HERMAN   Unh.

JUNIOR   I have to find my new fella.

(He is about to knock on Jean Genet.)

HERMAN   Unnnnhhhnnnnhhhh!

JUNIOR   Not this one? Upstairs?

(He runs upstairs and is about to knock on Marcel Proust.)

HERMAN   Unnnnnnnnnnnhhhhhhhhhhh!

JUNIOR   Not this one either? Thanks, Mr. Harrod. I owe you one. *(He knocks on the door of* FOPPY'S *room.)* I hope you're still all excited because I am and I can't wait. *(The door is locked.)* Sweetie—open up!

MAYOR'S VOICE   One second, I'm dressing.

JUNIOR   I don't want you dressed.

MAYOR'S VOICE   One second, I'm undressing.

JUNIOR   Hurry up, hurry up, hurry hurry hurry up! I'm in love with you.

(The MAYOR, *in boxer shorts with an apple pattern, starts opening the door, just as* FOPPY *comes out of Marcel Proust.)*

FOPPY   Stop in the name of love!

*(*FOPPY *pushes the* MAYOR *back in.)*

FOPPY   He's not the one! *(Slamming the door)*

(Marcel Proust's door opens a crack.)

MRS. POTENTATE'S VOICE   Someone's coming!

FOPPY   *(Closing the door in her face)* Don't know where, don't know when! *(To* JUNIOR*)* Go back to your room!

JUNIOR   You sound just like my mother.

MRS. POTENTATE'S VOICE   Has he come yet?

FOPPY   Not yet. Not yet. *(To* JUNIOR*)* I am your mother.

> (GILBERT *comes out of the kitchen, heads toward Oscar Wilde.)*

GILBERT   *(to* HERMAN*)* You're Herman Harrod. I've got your number. *(Goes into Oscar Wilde.)*

> (FOPPY *gets* JUNIOR *downstairs.)*

MRS. POTENTATE'S VOICE   *(Singing)* "God save our Gracious Queen . . ."

JUNIOR   Ma's in there!

FOPPY   On television. She's doing one of her cultural evenings with that handsome Marvin Hamlisch.

JUNIOR   That was the Mayor of our largest northeastern city!

FOPPY   It wasn't Sonny Bono.

JUNIOR   Where's Gilbert? First Son must warn First Love!

FOPPY   Into the kitchen. Your love is in the kitchen.

> *(He manages to get* JUNIOR *into the kitchen, when the* MAYOR *comes out, carrying suitcase and Gap bag.)*

MAYOR   I shall not stay unsatisfied inside this brothel one more second. I admit defeat. I can't keep it up anymore.

MRS. POTENTATE'S VOICE "Send her victorious, Happy and glorious . . ."

MAYOR The exterminator's a British woman?

FOPPY Just like Margaret Thatcher. *(Pushing MAYOR into Jean Genet)* Go in here! Temporarily.

MAYOR I want to go out there. Permanently.

(FOPPY *gets him into Genet, then rushes to* HERMAN.)

MRS. POTENTATE'S VOICE "God save the Queen. . . ."

MAYOR *(Rushing out)* There's a girl sleeping in there!

FOPPY Good! You're not gay!

MAYOR *(Meaning* HERMAN*)* I told you I didn't want that one!

FOPPY I've got another one. He'll be here in a minute. Get ready for him. Get ready to meet your combination Rob Lowe and Matt Dillon. Get ready to meet Mr. Right.

MAYOR There's a sleeping girl in there and a passed-out man out here. And I thought I had a drug problem in Appleberg.

FOPPY He's a combination Tom Selleck and Mark Harmon before they got married. You must stay hidden until you hear the magic word.

MAYOR Which is?

FOPPY Rudolph Giuliani.

(The MAYOR *goes into Genet and slams the door.*)

FOPPY Help thy neighbor, the Bible said. Right the wrongs of the world, Mother Teresa said. God bless

New Columbia, Kate Smith said. God bless mother-
fucking New Columbia, Whoopi Goldberg said . . .

HERMAN   Unnnnnnnhhhhh.

FOPPY   You would be alive. Is that good for me or bad?
Can you run outside to take the nearest subway? Can
we talk?

HERMAN   Unnnnhhhhhh.

FOPPY   Where is your goddamned tape!

HERMAN   Unnnnhhhh.

FOPPY   I do not understand "Unnnnhhhh." You got me
into this. Because of you I face imminent death. Oh,
what's the use, all you can say is "Unnnnhhhh."

HERMAN   Unnnhh. *(He moves his hand.)*

FOPPY   *(Rushing to find and give him paper and pen)* The
fickle finger of fate? *(As HERMAN writes something)* My
God! There is a God! He's still alive?

HERMAN   Unnnh.

FOPPY   Where?

> (HERMAN *starts to pass out again.* FOPPY *locates
> his coke.)*

FOPPY   Where? Where is he?

HERMAN   Unnnnhhhh.

FOPPY   That does not help me. (HERMAN *writes some
more, then passes out again.)* The moving finger writes
and having writ moves on.

> *(He rushes to the phone. While he talks, he pulls a
> painting on hinges away from the wall; a reel-to-reel
> tape recorder is revealed. He prepares it.)*

FOPPY   Operator, I need the number of . . . in Pasadena
. . . is there an old fart's home, folk's home, for movie
old people, you know, alta cockers. . . . My dear, thank
you! Don't let anyone ever tell you again your service
stinks. *(He dials again, as he turns on tape recorder.)* Make
way, Kitty Kelley, here comes Foppy!

(GILBERT *comes out of Oscar Wilde, dressed.)*

GILBERT   *(To* FOPPY*)* If we had Trudi's tape, we could
be free and rich and live anywhere we want to. . . .

FOPPY   You've worked all that out, have you? *(On the
phone)* Mr. Thau, please.

GILBERT   Junior will never have to worry about Mommy
and Daddy again.

FOPPY   Well, wheel his chair to the phone!

(HERMAN *has tried to stand up, and* GILBERT
helps lean him against the wall by Oscar Wilde.)

GILBERT   I'll be a hero.

FOPPY   Well, don't they have phones in Intensive Care?!

GILBERT   We could live on Fifth Avenue. Overlooking
the park.

FOPPY   Well, hold the phone up to the respirator!

GILBERT   Maybe Bessie could lend us her boyfriend-in-
jail's house at Westhampton Beach.

FOPPY   Benny, *was machst du? (He turns on tape recorder.)*

*(Another black-gloved hand reaches out from Oscar
Wilde and covers* HERMAN*'s mouth and pulls him
into Oscar Wilde.)*

HERMAN   Unnnnnhhhh!

FOPPY   I cannot tell you how glad I am you're still alive.

HERMAN   Unnnnhhhh!

FOPPY   Will you shut up! No, not you, Benny! I caught you before you're almost dead? Before you go to meet your maker, I know you want to go and make him with a clear conscience. . . . Let's talk about First Mommy.

GILBERT   Make who with a clear what? Who are you talking to? I hope you're not playing a dangerous game.

FOPPY   Benny, I love you, Benny! Yes, I know you're not a fairy! But you are, Benny, you are, you're the good fairy. . . .

(He hangs up the phone and takes the tape from the recorder and rushes upstairs.)

FOPPY   *(To GILBERT, as he goes)* Our redeemer liveth. Although he didn't sound so hot. This scene requires a change of outfit. Something more Joan Crawford. I have it. I have it! I've found my weapon! My instrument! My dick of death! *(Goes into his bedroom, slamming door.)*

GILBERT   Wow!

(GILBERT picks up a pair of HERMAN's handcuffs. He throws them giddily over his left shoulder with his right hand. The MAYOR peeks out of Jean Genet, thinks the coast is clear. He is dressed in a version of what he thinks is sexually alluring: Levi's that are brand new and stiff and too big for him, a cowboy shirt, a red bandanna around his neck, plus a yellow kerchief in his right hip pocket. He wears cowboy boots like a young girl who can't quite manage her first high heels. The MAYOR and GILBERT back into each other.)

MAYOR   Howdy, True Love. You!

GILBERT   Me?

> (GILBERT *is terrified, and keeps evading the*
> MAYOR.*)*

MAYOR   You can of worms!

GILBERT   Me can of worms.

MAYOR   You torpid rodent.

GILBERT   Me what rodent?

MAYOR   You lustless feldsheimer.

GILBERT   I am not lustless.

MAYOR   *(Finally grabbing him)* Your repellent physique
disgusts me. To touch your offensive skin. And hold
your obnoxious body against my obnoxious body. And
push you against this wall. And strangle your precious
concave chest. Oh my god why why why why how how
how how what what what what is happening to me?
My groin runneth over. My base private parts nauseat-
ingly worship you abhorrently. My lovely hands and
my magnificent brain want to kiss you kill you kiss you
kill you, oh Gilbert, my loathesome Gilbert . . . *(He is
both kissing him and mauling him.)*

GILBERT   Oh, Mayor, my mayor . . .

MAYOR   I told you you could always call me May. How
could you have left me?!

GILBERT   You sent your goons to kill me.

MAYOR   That's right. I did.

GILBERT   You told me real estate interests would kill me
if I croaked!

MAYOR   That's right. They would.

GILBERT   You said anyone working in Sex and Germs who even said the word AIDS would be fired.

MAYOR   That's right. You were.

GILBERT   I could never love anyone in the closet.

MAYOR   You're right. I'm not gay.

(*The* MAYOR *kisses and mauls him some more as they continue. . . .*)

GILBERT   We had no future.

MAYOR   No future? I got reelected, didn't I? And I'll do it again. And again. And again and again and again. Oooohhhh . . . Aaaaahhhhhh . . .

GILBERT   How can you get reelected when you've had a hundred indictments against your staff?

MAYOR   One hundred and ten. Always appear to be honest with figures. You won't succeed. But try.

GILBERT   You would call me from your office sometimes four times a day.

MAYOR   Maybe three times at the most.

GILBERT   You'd say, "Why dontcha come over for a tid-dyly-do," and I would and we would and two seconds afterward you would scream, "Get outta my life, I'm not gay!" But always, one, two, three, at the most four days later . . .

MAYOR   Two, three weeks.

GILBERT   . . . you'd call again and whisper, "Please come and fanky fanky," and I'd say, "But you said," and you'd say . . .

MAYOR   Never mind what I said.

GILBERT   And I'd think that was so sweet.

MAYOR   The Mayor of New Columbia's largest north-eastern city is not sweet!

GILBERT   And then you sent emissaries of death to kill me.

MAYOR   Oh, Gilbert, just hearing your whiny voice, just looking into your dribbly eyes, just feeling your dumpy body, I've got lover's nuts.

GILBERT   *Lover.* How long I longed to hear you say that word.

MAYOR   It doesn't mean anything. It's generic. Like Kleenex and Jell-O.

GILBERT   There you go avoiding my needs again. My shrink said your bite is worse than your bark.

MAYOR   You told a shrink! I'll enter the psychiatric literature.

GILBERT   He said you were definitely not good relationship material.

MAYOR   You feel so fetid!

GILBERT   He said you were a very confused and mixed-up person.

MAYOR   You feel so fetid and good and fetid and good and I love you hate you love you hate you love you hate you . . .

GILBERT   *(Pushing him away)* I am a conflicted man in pain.

MAYOR   *(Trying to move but unable to)* I am a man in pain!

GILBERT   And that bimbo slut Hiram took my place in your pants!

MAYOR   I was just waiting for my dick to find you. Hiding from me, afraid I would tear you limb from limb into the tiniest measly bitty itty pieces of flesh. Oh flesh. Oh oh oh oh oh flesh.

GILBERT   The real estate interests didn't want to encase me in cement?

MAYOR   Donny Trump? Ivana will throw you a party.

GILBERT   I misunderstood you, May.

(GILBERT *starts responding to the* MAYOR. *He is particularly perplexed and pleased by the* MAYOR's *bulging crotch.*)

GILBERT   Oh, May, you're so hard. You've grown!

MAYOR   Let's get to a bed, we got to get to a bed . . .

GILBERT   I don't remember you being so big and hard. Did you send away for that kit?

MAYOR   . . . we must get somewhere fast pronto schnell . . .

GILBERT   A tisket a tasket . . .

MAYOR   We got to hit something to lie down on or it will be tooooooooo . . . late. I mussed my . . . Thank God I wore four pairs of underpants.

GILBERT   Remember when you had to wear that diaper, too?

MAYOR   So you miserable perverted twat, how much do you want?! I will not be blackmailed! I always get even—that is my inflexible rule. I am not gay! I will not do anything to rid your fairy community of your filthy diseases and to all your habits and desires I say feh!

GILBERT   (*Still investigating his jeans*) But the Surgeon General says this is going to happen to everybody. You're still hard.

MAYOR The Surgeon General! It's very unattractive when an older man becomes so obsessed with sex.

GILBERT *(Managing to extract the tape from the* MAYOR's *crotch)* A green and yellow basket. *(He holds it at arm's length, delicately.)*

MAYOR Give me that tape! *(He starts chasing* GILBERT.*)* I must have it! I could become Potentate-in-Chief.

GILBERT The tape! I could become Mrs. Potentate.

MAYOR I could expose this awful canker in Daddy's asshole and become a national hero and take its place.

GILBERT I could become Mrs. Junior Potentate.

MAYOR Will my life never be free of crooks making deals! You fork over that tape or I'll sic Mario B. on you—no, Mario's been convicted, I'll sic Donny M. on you. . . . I've still got Meade, Geoffrey, Lester, Michael, Marvin, Anthony, Jay, John, Richard, Vito, Victor . . . I'm all alone.

GILBERT And still as much of a gonif twit as ever.

MAYOR I give you my tongue and you spit it back at me! You are low and wretched scum of the earth and I will see to it that you are sent up to the top of the World Trade Center and like a bird turd, dropped. *(He has caught him again and they go through their physical contortions again, at the same time as they each try to get or keep the tape.)* Oh, oh oh oh oh you repellent sexual obsessive object of putrescence and desire oh oh oh oh no no no no NO NO NO NO NO!

(JUNIOR comes out of the kitchen.)

JUNIOR My true love in another's arms!

GILBERT I can explain!

JUNIOR My heart is broken . . .

GILBERT   I was only trying to grab his powerful tape!

JUNIOR   . . . for the third time today.

GILBERT   You're much more powerful to me!

MAYOR   My God, you're the First Son! *(Seeing how cute*
JUNIOR *is)* Can a dapper, wiser . . . older man offer
guidance and assistance?

JUNIOR   You love another!

GILBERT   I love also only you better!

JUNIOR   I never want to see you again.

(The doorway to Marcel Proust opens.)

MRS. POTENTATE   Foppy . . .

FOPPY   Yes?

MRS. POTENTATE   I am tired of vamping till ready.

MAYOR   The exterminator is the First Lady!

JUNIOR   Ma is here!

*(JUNIOR, GILBERT, and the MAYOR rush to go
into rooms to hide. But the doorways to Genet and
Wilde are locked. They run into the closet under the
balcony. MRS. POTENTATE starts down the
stairs, fully dressed as when she arrived.
EUSTACIA comes out of the kitchen.)*

MRS. POTENTATE   This must be remembered as a
Golden Age.

FOPPY   *(Coming out of his bedroom wearing his most dramatic
robe yet)* This will be remembered as *the* Golden Age.
Eustacia, prepare for high tea!

EUSTACIA   Mr. Foppy, there is not one crumb of anything to eat left in this whole house.

FOPPY   Then she shall eat cake.

(JUNIOR, GILBERT, *and the* MAYOR *come
rushing out of the closet.*)

JUNIOR   What are we going to do?

FOPPY   Trust me. Go back in the closet. (*He pushes them
back in.*)

MRS. POTENTATE   Whoever the traitor is who betrayed
me, off with his head when he presents it. Everyone is
against me. Everyone is playing gotcha. I don't like growing old. I don't like going back to the Palace hungry.

FOPPY   So coitus interruptus.

MRS. POTENTATE   So coitus not-even startus.

FOPPY   (*To* EUSTACIA) Serve tea. Hot tea, iced tea,
Mr. T, serve anything!

EUSTACIA   Just remember, women get meaner when
they thought they were going to get it and we didn't.

MRS. POTENTATE   Amen.

FOPPY   That is not a characteristic exclusive to your sex.

EUSTACIA   Then go out and give one to the gipper. (*She
goes into kitchen.*)

MRS. POTENTATE   If it's not one hole to plug up, it's
another. I wonder what my dearest friend, Queen Eliz-
abeth, would have done if Mr. Profumo and his friends
were all available on home videotapes. Do you think
anybody even remembers the Profumo Affair?

(EUSTACIA *comes out of the kitchen with the tray
on a stand, with an assortment of any old thing,
including a large bottle of instant tea.*)

EUSTACIA   A sex scandal that brought down the British government.

MRS. POTENTATE   No. Nobody remembers the Profumo Affair.

EUSTACIA   An innocent man was sacrificed and a guilty man protected because he had the right connections.

FOPPY   No, nobody remembers that it was two bimby sluts who brought down Betty Windsor's government.

MRS. POTENTATE   Two bimby sluts?

FOPPY and EUSTACIA   Two bimby sluts.

EUSTACIA   (*Offering tea*) Earl Grey. Prince of Wales. Princess Vye's Hemlock.

MRS. POTENTATE   (*Taking tea*) Thank you, Eukanuba.

EUSTACIA   Eustacia. Eustacia Vye.

MRS. POTENTATE   Of course. Eukanuba is dog food.

(EUSTACIA *plops all the instant tea into a cup, causing clouds, and hands the overflowing mess to* MRS. POTENTATE.)

FOPPY   Really, my Barbara Jordan! . . .

MRS. POTENTATE   Spare me Grimms' Fairy Tales, my Noel Coward. . . .

(FOPPY *motions to* EUSTACIA *to leave, which she does. During the following confrontation,* EUSTACIA'*s face can be seen peeking through the kitchen door, and* JUNIOR'*s head sticking out of the closet—to hear all. . . .*)

FOPPY   Then try Foppy's. My Capitol Concubine, you have always surrounded yourself with the sensitive, the

gifted, the amusing. . . . You have even allowed yours
truly to be among your most trusted confidantes. . . .
You do remember all your dear mother's dear lesbian
friends who were so helpful to you? Your godmother
—the Queen of the Hollywood dykes. Your Broadway
career—such as it was . . .

MRS. POTENTATE   Such as it was?

FOPPY   Such as it was, and due to lesbian stars. Then
there is hope, my old friend.

MRS. POTENTATE   I am beginning to feel not so
friendly.

FOPPY   Oh, my Supreme Arbiter, my Dictator of Right
and Wrong, I have been thinking of how happy we were
in those old days, where we were young and carefree,
swinging along Hollywood and Vine, gallivanting at
homes and studios, with powerful moguls and stars,
like Benny Thau. . . .

MRS. POTENTATE   Benny Thau? Are you pressing me
again for the name of a lawyer?

FOPPY   There is nothing illegal about the head of MGM
receiving what he has nominated as the best blow jobs
he ever had.

MRS. POTENTATE   Foppy the Lion is almost dead.

FOPPY   It's a shame. It was once considered such a great
art. And you such a promising player.

MRS. POTENTATE   My Beatrice Lillie, there are fairies
at the bottom of my garden.

FOPPY   You were a very ambitious starlet, my Eve Har-
rington.

MRS. POTENTATE   *"Were,"* my Suddenly Sounding Ad-
dison De Witless?

FOPPY   Ah, I have taught you too well. Yes, it's always been mandatory for you to get ahead. Now historians will be able to fill in the bank with: whose.

MRS. POTENTATE   You are treading on the tenderest toes.

FOPPY   You were kneeling on the sorest knees.

MRS. POTENTATE   Your head is heading toward High Noon.

FOPPY   Yes, every Saturday at High Noon, Benny Thau's head met your head. You have always worshiped at the feet of power.

MRS. POTENTATE   Since when have you become so interested in the politics of power, my Benedict Arnold?

FOPPY   Since you became so inextricably interested in fucking my people, my Linda Lovelace.

MRS. POTENTATE   Then be careful that you don't go too far, my Julius Rosenberg.

FOPPY   I go too far? From your very first screen test with Spencer Tracy, you have given new meaning to the expression "Life is better under the Republicans."

MRS. POTENTATE   Spencer Tracy was a drunk who could never get it up.

FOPPY   And so you stooped to conquer.

MRS. POTENTATE   Oh, you silly poofter faggot queen, you now go too far, too.

FOPPY   Two? Yes, Benny reminded me he had you service two: Spencer Tracy's and Clark Gable's.

MRS. POTENTATE   Clark Gable was insignificant.

FOPPY   But it happened many nights you made him so much larger.

MRS. POTENTATE   The sequel to mutiny on the bounty is gone with the wind.

FOPPY   Or guess who's coming to dinner.

MRS. POTENTATE   Do you know the penalty for exposing official secrets about an official?

FOPPY   It depends on whether you're trying to be Betsy Ross or Betsy Bloomingdale.

MRS. POTENTATE   You aren't either, my Sweet Betsy from Kike.

FOPPY   But, my Ilse Koch, I have located dear Benny. *(Displays the tape of their phone conversation.)*

MRS. POTENTATE   You, too, are into tapes, my Tricky Dickie? Georgetown is afflicted with a plague of tapeworm.

FOPPY   A plague, to be sure. Let us try not to allow history to punish us too much, my Barbara Tuchman.

MRS. POTENTATE   Do I sense a negotiation transpiring?

FOPPY   You do.

MRS. POTENTATE   It is a tawdry one.

FOPPY   Filled with junk bonds, my Drexel Burnham. Daddy has ignored all action on AIDS. With three official reports on this deadly matter, is it not time you taught him how to read? With your own son at such high risk.

MRS. POTENTATE   So you are going to tell the world about Junior?

JUNIOR   *(Jumping out)* Junior is going to tell the world about Junior.

MRS. POTENTATE   You are naked!

JUNIOR   For all the world to see.

MRS. POTENTATE So everybody knows?

JUNIOR Aw, come on, Ma. I've always known. So have you. I was born this way.

MRS. POTENTATE You were not born this way! You were just too young when I took you to see *The Red Shoes*.

FOPPY Oh, come now, dear. A mother always knows. Everybody knows.

JUNIOR Is that why you locked me up in my room all those years? So you could blow your wild oats? That's not being a very good Ma, Ma.

FOPPY Now. I also want Daddy to issue an Executive Order, then propose legislation prohibiting discrimination on the basis of sexual orientation. . . .

JUNIOR Men are going to marry men! If we have anything to say about it.

MRS. POTENTATE Let me tell you, you are never ever going to have anything to say about it. *(To* FOPPY*)* So this is your price?

JUNIOR Hey, Ma, it's not such a high price.

FOPPY And as long as we are negotiating so successfully, my Sandra Day O'Connor, Daddy must also petition for the Supreme Tribunal to rehear that wretched wrongful case that has made your own son illegal. Your own flesh and blood.

JUNIOR Oh, Uncle Foppy, I'm so proud of you. I can't thank you enough. Our brothers and sisters can't thank you enough!

FOPPY I am overdue for Kennedy Center honors.

MRS. POTENTATE You're getting married in the morning.

JUNIOR   I'm never going to marry a woman.

MRS. POTENTATE   Is it too late to marry him off to an understanding older woman or a dyke? In the old days, all the dykes made movies. Now they play tennis. If it's not one kind of damage control, it's another. Uncle Lyn, Uncle Michael, Uncle Donny, Uncle Ed, Uncle Herman. Now you. Why can't men keep it in their pants? Your mother has found you a tennis player.

(JUNIOR *goes and pulls* GILBERT *out of the closet.*)

JUNIOR   Mom—I want you to meet your new son-in-law.

GILBERT   Junior, I'm sorry about our fight, and I love you and I'll live anywhere with you, even Appleberg, but be careful, not all beasts are men.

MRS. POTENTATE   (*To* FOPPY) And you think I'm going to let you get away with this! (*To* GILBERT) Enunciate your name with clarity.

GILBERT   Oh, Ma'am. I don't know what to say. I'm so honored. I love your son.

MRS. POTENTATE   How do you wish to die?

GILBERT   I don't wish to die. I just loved your husband's first wife in *Johnny Belinda*.

MRS. POTENTATE   I repeat my question.

GILBERT   But she won an Oscar.

MRS. POTENTATE   For playing deaf and dumb.

JUNIOR   Mom—why are you such a hypocrite?

FOPPY   Why does familiarity breed such contempt?

JUNIOR   At least I'm trying not to deceive the world. I haven't told them I was one thing while all the time I was another. I haven't denied who I was and am. I haven't tried to punish anyone for who and what they are. If you don't let me dance with Gilbert I'm going to tell the world.

MRS. POTENTATE   Tell the world . . . what . . . specifically?

JUNIOR   That the First Family has the worst family life since the Addams Family. And not John Quincy, Mother, Charles.

EUSTACIA   *(Entering with champagne and glasses)* It sounds like mother-fucking time. It's time to celebrate.

MRS. POTENTATE   *(Turning on EUSTACIA)* Beware!

EUSTACIA   I'm not afraid of you.

MRS. POTENTATE   You should be. I'll take your drugs away!

EUSTACIA   Thank you, thank you, glory hallelujah!

MRS. POTENTATE   Oh, not those drugs. Take all of those drugs you want. I mean health care, medicine, education—that's a drug! And abortion! I've taken away all your abortions. So you can never get out of your filthy rut, with your voracious appetite for sex, and children, and sex, and more children, and more sex . . .

FOPPY   Really, my Mad Scene from Lucia!

EUSTACIA   Proud African Intellect Strangles Mommie Dearest.

JUNIOR   Dad passed around like cheesecake . . .

FOPPY   Fruitcake.

JUNIOR   Mom made her career on her back.

FOPPY   More or less.

JUNIOR   Maybe it's time for you to go home and talk this all out with Daddy.

FOPPY   Before you steal home, we must settle our grand
design for our new history, my Clare Loose Tooth.

MRS. POTENTATE   Home! Home! I've swallowed enough!
What do you faggots know of home?! (*To* JUNIOR) Tell
the world? You think the world cares? You think the world
wants to know my son is gay? My daughter is a drugged-
out hippie? My son and his family are estranged? I am a
married woman and a mother! Everyone normal is married! You can't or won't get married, so you're not normal.
Daddy is the most powerful Potentate since Jesus. No one
wants to know anything juicy about Jesus!

FOPPY   Dishonor is the bitter part of squalor. But I have
yet to play my ace.

(FOPPY *runs to the front door, throws it open,
rushes out, and screams.*)

FOPPY   Media! Are you out there, Media! Can you
hear me, Max Frankel, Tom Brokaw, Dan Rather, Ted
Koppel . . .

(*But during the above, the noise of sirens has
increased in closeness and in volume.* FOPPY *is
bathed in searchlight. Two arms hold up guns to
either side of his temple. He is forced to come back in.*)

MRS. POTENTATE   You amateur. Me a supporting
player? You are playing opposite a star!

MAYOR   (*Entering*) Enough of this hoity-toity. Permit me
to introduce you to my ward and soon-to-be adopted
son, Mr. Gilbert Perch, who is in the business of White
Palace sex videotapes.

FOPPY   You've got the tape?

MAYOR   (*Giving tape to* GILBERT) Show her my powerful
tape.

GILBERT   Here is his powerful tape. . . .

MRS. POTENTATE   And where is Herman Harrod?

EUSTACIA   *(Realizing)* The dead Herman's gone.

JUNIOR   He wasn't dead. He spoke to me. Sort of.

MRS. POTENTATE   Herman Harrod will be found in a bed in St. John's Hospital. Dead.

GILBERT   Where's Trudi!

MRS. POTENTATE   That's her room.

(GILBERT *rushes to Jean Genet. The door is no longer locked. He goes in and comes back out holding a baseball bat.*)

GILBERT   Trudi's dead.

FOPPY   Trudi's dead?

MRS. POTENTATE   She has been clobbered to death with a Louisville Slugger.

FOPPY   Trudi's been murdered? It's all becoming too unsavory to the aesthete's eye. My Holy Mother . . .

MRS. POTENTATE   *(To* FOPPY*)* I'm not ready for you yet. *(To* GILBERT*)* Do you play baseball?

GILBERT   Trudi's been murdered?

MRS. POTENTATE   Of course you play baseball. Are you a good boy who loves your mother more than life itself?

GILBERT   Trudi's been murdered?

MRS. POTENTATE   Of course you love your mother more than life itself. Does she live in the luxury you wish and dream for her?

GILBERT   She lives a humble life in a rent-controlled apartment in Greenwich Village.

MAYOR   I thought I evicted you from that apartment.

MRS. POTENTATE   While you are in prison for the murder of Trudi Tunick, your beloved mother will receive great sums of money.

JUNIOR   You can't do this!

MAYOR   No, you can't do this.

GILBERT   I knew I loved you both. Nevertheless, I'm still scared shitless.

FOPPY   She would perform any act to get ahead. Now she's gone down on history.

MRS. POTENTATE   Gilbert Perch, you were found with the body of Trudi Tunick, holding that baseball bat with your own fingerprints.

(With a handkerchief, MRS. POTENTATE *takes the baseball bat.)*

MRS. POTENTATE   And with this filthy, dirty, vile, putrid, disgusting sex tape. *(She pops it in her bag.)* Poof! All gone! *(Separating* JUNIOR *and* GILBERT*)* Poofs! All gone!

JUNIOR   Oh, no, you don't! This time I'm fighting back! You're not going to lock me in my room anymore. . . . You can't do this!

MRS. POTENTATE   *(To* GILBERT*)* . . . and you are the Mayor's . . . mistress? Mister?

MAYOR   Yes, she can do this. It has been my experience that it's never too late to marry an understanding older woman or a dyke.

GILBERT   Help me, Junior . . . I need your strength. . . .

JUNIOR I love him! And our love is good and pure and eternal and everlasting and forever and ever. . . .

MRS. POTENTATE No, you won't tell the world. No, you won't become a dancer. Or your people will be quarantined, put into camps, after mandatory testing, with no more research, or treatments, or insurance, or jobs, allowed to die. . . .

EUSTACIA The song is ended.

MRS. POTENTATE And Daddy and I are so very very close to dearest George and Barbara. . . .

EUSTACIA But the melody lingers on.

MRS. POTENTATE (To JUNIOR) And you will get married, or you'll never dance on "Saturday Night Live" alive.

GILBERT Mommie, I always promised you I would take care of you.

MAYOR Gilbert Perch, you have betrayed my trust in you, you pig.

MRS. POTENTATE And darling Fopp, who will invite you to any parties? Carolina, Chessy, Mica, Pat, Marella, Nan, Louise, Estee, Ann, Judy, Slim, Betsy, Jackie, me . . .

EUSTACIA (To audience) Old Georgetown saying: if you dig grave for enemy, dig two—one for self.

MRS. POTENTATE (Using her phone) KY 123 to KY 4567. Sheilasuellen, inform all media that writing about this is a no-no and a grossly punishable offense. And call Betsy, tell her we're celebrating. I'll wear my new Galanos and she must wear her old Blass. And call Jean, Virginia, Marion, Martha, Leonore, Harriet, and Mary Jane, and tell them to join us tomorrow at Le Cirque in Appleberg. With the Mayor. (To FOPPY) How much do you love me?

FOPPY   How deep is the ocean? *(Handing over Benny Thau's tape)*

MRS. POTENTATE   *(On phone)* And Mr. Schwartz. *(She's pushed another number.)* Daddums, it's all done. I've saved our reign for history. *(Hangs up.)* Daddy's on TV.

(The MAYOR *rushes to turn on the TV. Everyone goes to watch. Lights down.* EUSTACIA *is picked up in a spotlight.)*

EUSTACIA   Gilbert Perch confessed to the murder of Trudi Tunick. If you can believe that, you'll believe anything. He's in the prison nut house, and he's come down with AIDS. I hope Junior's health is okay. And his wife's. No, the police didn't come inside to investigate the murder at all. It's Marilyn all over again. And Dorothy. And Chappaquiddick. The Mayor's running for another term. If you can vote for him, you'll vote for anybody. Mr. Foppy and me—we're still together. Nobody would believe our story. It doesn't have a happy ending. Daddy only approves of happy endings. If you've been in as many bad movies as he has, after a while I guess you believe in happy endings. After all, it turned out fine for him thirty-nine times at Warner Brothers. Mr. Foppy says this country's philosophy is, "I love Mommy and Daddy as long as they don't tell me about the dark." My philosophy is . . . well, as another old Georgetown broad once said, "If you haven't got anything good to say about anyone, come sit with me." Yes, it's morning again in New Columbia. Now, I'm afraid. Now, I know too much, too. Now so do you. Now what are you going to do?

The End